Isle of Man
WILDLIFE

CONTRIBUTORS

Duncan Bridges (Manx Wildlife Trust),
Steve Crellin, Andree Dubbeldam (Manx
Wildlife Trust), Dr Karen Galtress (DEFA),
Jackie Hall (Manx Wildlife Trust), Kate
Hawkins (Manx National Heritage), Nick
Pinder (Curraghs Wildlife Park), Chris
Sharpe (Manx Bird Life), Eleanor Stone
(Manx Wildlife Trust)

Edited and compiled by
Trevor Barrett

Managing editor
Miles Cowsill

PHOTOGRAPHY
Miles Cowsill, Visit Isle of Man, Andree
Dubbeldam and Pete Hadfield
(www.manxbirdphotography.co.uk)

 Published by Lily Publications Ltd.,
PO Box 33, Ramsey, Isle of Man, IM99 4LP
Tel: +44 (0)1624 898446, Fax: +44 (0)1624 898449.
www.lilypublications.co.uk   lilypubs@manx.net

CONTENTS

A colourful display of thrift (sea pink) at Derbyhaven, where neighbouring Langness is excellent for birdwatching.

WILDLIFE ON THE LAND

THE CALF OF MAN

Managed by Manx National Heritage as a nature reserve and bird observatory, the Calf of Man seems on the face of it to be a tranquil place – an ideal escape from the demands of everyday modern life. And yet, for much of the year, it's a hive of activity. Whether you come to watch the wildlife, or to walk amongst spectacular scenery, or are a volunteer conservationist, there's always something happening here.

In May, carpets of bluebells scent the air and violets nestle amongst the new bracken fronds. Above the rocky shore at South Harbour, spring and early summer see the coastal grassland dotted with spring squill, sea campion, sea-spurreys, English stonecrop and bird's-foot trefoil. Dark green fritillary butterflies especially appreciate the abundant thrift, a nectar source in late June.

A walk up to the observatory from South Harbour takes you past the old mill pond, where marsh plants such as round-leaved sundew, marsh St John's-wort and marsh pennywort thrive and where you may spot dragonflies and damselflies. At wet flushes and ditches around the island you can find the diminutive bog pimpernel and patches of sphagnum mosses and, if your luck's in, a wild orchid or two. The wild flowers have to contend with grazing from sheep and rabbits, so may be dwarfed or confined to places out of the reach of hungry herbivores.

From March until November, the old farmhouse in the centre of the island serves as the bird observatory headquarters, information centre and guest accommodation for up to eight people. Two wardens run the bird recording and ringing programme, provide advice to visitors, and maintain equipment and facilities around the island. Birds are caught in mist nets and Heligoland traps and, if they're not too busy, the wardens are happy to demonstrate the harmless process of ringing.

On the migration route for many summer and winter birds, the Calf of Man was well known amongst ornithologists long before it was established as a bird observatory in 1959, by which time farming had become largely unviable. Up until that point the island had been variously occupied by farming families, lighthouse keepers, military

garrisons, hermits and fugitives. Their legacy lies in the historic buildings and the landscape features they left behind. Around the farmhouse the dry stone walls enclosing the fields are still maintained to contain the Loaghtan sheep, used today in grassland management.

At the top of the cliffs on the south-west side, two 1819 Stevenson lighthouses, the 1960s lighthouse complex between them and the Chicken Rock lighthouse built a kilometre out to sea in 1875, all attest to the dangers faced by seamen in the past. Though no doubt saving many human lives, these lights were a death trap for many birds migrating at night. Confused by the glare, they dashed themselves to death against the towers. Hopefully, in line with modern lighthouse operation, the restored and currently functioning light on Chicken Rock no longer causes such calamity.

The Calf is well known as the place where Manx shearwaters were first systematically described by Francis Willoughby. His account of the 'Mank

The Calf of Man is known not only for its birdlife but also for its lighthouse heritage.

The Bird Observatory (above left), founded in 1959, is based in what was once the Calf's main farmhouse.

puffin' was published in 1678, after his death, and the name Manx shearwater adopted about a century later. The once huge colony of these seabirds, known by local people as 'puffins', used to be an important economic resource for the Isle of Man. Nesting in burrows, each pair of shearwaters raises a single chick until it is big and fat enough to be abandoned in its burrow by the parent birds, which return to sea. The chick goes on to fledge and leaves the nest about two weeks later.

From as early as medieval times until the end of the 1700s, people harvested the fat chicks by pulling them from their burrows, killing them in their thousands for their meat and oil. Culling was merciless, and could have contributed to the catastrophic collapse of the breeding colony, though an invasion of brown rats (often called 'longtails') from a shipwreck in the 1780s is traditionally blamed for its demise. Though they have never recovered their former numbers, Manx shearwaters nest in several

small colonies today, closely monitored and guarded from predatory rats by the wardens. Shearwaters spend their days feeding out at sea, coming back to land and their nests under cover of darkness to avoid the attentions of gulls. Their eerie cries as they fly overhead are unmistakeable today, but were said to have scared at least one Viking chieftain who, in 1014, took the nocturnal cacophony to be an ill omen and sailed shortly after to his defeat at the Battle of Clontarf in Ireland.

Though the emblematic Manx shearwaters are a major focus of the wildlife conservation effort on the Calf, the island is also well known for another charismatic species – the chough. With safe places to nest and plenty of short, well-manured (by sheep or rabbits) turf to probe for grubs, choughs thrive on the Calf and the adjacent mainland coast. They are present throughout the year on the Calf and are a conservation success story, thanks to local efforts to monitor them and manage the landscape in their favour. The raven is another crow species which nests on the Calf. Though it has a mixed reception from sheep farmers these days, this magnificent bird is also a source of legend in the Isle of Man. The Vikings believed that ravens were associated with the Norse god Odin, who sent two of them out to gather knowledge of the world.

Nesting seabirds frequent the coast and cliffs of the Calf from about April until the end of July. The most inaccessible rock faces are occupied by common guillemots, razorbills, fulmars and kittiwakes, while nearer the foot of the cliffs and amongst the boulder fields are sizeable colonies of shags and a few pairs of black guillemots. Kittiwakes, dependent as they are on the availability of sand eels as food for their young, vary greatly in numbers and breeding success.

Colonies of herring gulls are on grassy cliff tops while the less common lesser black-backed gulls occupy the heath. Great black-backed gulls tend to nest amongst the rocks above the tide line. Puffins (the 'sea parrots' or 'poltrag' in Manx) have nested on the Calf in the past, but appear to struggle to breed nowadays. A few can be seen around the Calf in most years, though like the gannets diving offshore which commute from their nesting colonies in Scotland, they are most likely to be spotted out on the sea. Eider ducks, which have become increasingly common around the Isle of Man in recent years, attempt to nest regularly on the Calf, though their chicks have to run the gauntlet of the gulls. Another possible breeding species is the little storm petrel which, like the related Manx shearwater, spends its days feeding at sea and only comes to land during the breeding season under the cover of darkness. Both these species are ringed at night by the ornithological warden by use of sound recording lures and mist nets.

Coastal paths and harbour approaches are the best places from which to observe most of the seabirds, and you should not need to stray from the main routes. You won't fail to notice the oystercatchers, which will usually

A very appropriate bird's-eye view of the Calf of Man – as seen by its many avian inhabitants and migrants.

object noisily to your approach, but other waders may be more circumspect, such as the purple sandpipers, curlews, whimbrels and greenshanks passing by on their early-autumn migration. There is also a good chance of discretely observing grey seals hauled out on the rocky beaches or lazing about in the shallows, especially from above Cow Harbour, looking back across the Sound towards Kitterland and the main island.

The Calf provides a home or a stopping-off place for several birds of prey. Peregrines can usually be detected through their calls and might be spotted soaring over the cliffs. Long-eared and short-eared owls make hunting forays over to the Calf and occasionally nest here. Merlins, kestrels, sparrowhawks, buzzards, red kites, marsh harriers and even ospreys have been recorded passing through on migration. Amongst the birds most often seen by visitors are hen harriers. Despite being one of the most threatened bird species in the British Isles, hen harriers have done well on the Isle of Man and on the Calf, breeding and wintering here in relatively healthy numbers. Their habit of cruising low over the hunting ground makes them easy to recognise, especially the distinctive grey males.

Away from the coast, the most common birds encountered around the Calf in summer are those of heath, open grassland and scrub, such as wrens, linnets, wheatears, stonechats and meadow pipits. Around the observatory, swallows swoop for insects and nest in roof spaces. However, the observatory really comes into its own during the spring and autumn migrations, when the trees and shrubs around the garden and buildings attract birds pausing to rest and feed. Willow warblers, chiffchaffs, goldcrests, chaffinches and greenfinches are amongst the most frequently-ringed species, along with blackbirds, robins, redwings, fieldfares, song thrushes, tits, swallows,

Chicken Rock lighthouse, working to guide ships through the treacherous waters to the south of the Calf.

martins, other warblers and, less commonly, spotted flycatchers and siskins. More rarely caught and ringed species include firecrests, whinchats and common crossbills.

For the connoisseur, there is always a chance of spotting a rarity or two. Highlights in the fairly recent past have included hoopoe, golden oriole and red-backed shrike. A complete list of the birds recorded and ringed on the Calf is available from the observatory wardens or Manx National Heritage (see contact details on page 11).

Sea watching can be very rewarding at certain times of year for those equipped with binoculars or telescope. Try the area above Cow Harbour in the north-east of the island or the west coast between the lighthouses and Caigher Point. Amongst the passing shearwaters may be a sooty or Balearic shearwater or two, or one of the skuas. Unusual gulls such as sabine's or Iceland, can appear, as can red-throated or great northern divers, or ducks such as

From the Isle of Man mainland the Calf is just across the Sound.

pochard, common scoters, golden-eye or red-breasted merganser.

In early summer, from the Calf's higher viewpoints, you could be lucky enough to catch a glimpse of the dorsal fin of a basking shark. Sometimes, several of these magnificent gentle giants congregate to feed on plankton swarms at the northern end of the Sound, where they are in plain view of the Calf and the Sound café. For patient sea watchers there may be the reward of a sighting of porpoises, dolphins or – exceptionally – even an orca or minke whale.

A leisurely walk around the Calf is a very satisfying way in which to pass a couple of hours or so, but if you have to catch the boat make sure you leave enough time to get back to the harbour. Time – and more crucially tide – wait for no man!

Day visitors to the Calf of Man are welcomed, but you're advised to check boat availability from Port Erin quayside. If you wish to book overnight accommodation, or special trips to the Calf, you should contact the Calf Bookings Officer at Manx National Heritage (telephone 01624 648000 or e-mail enquiries@mnh.gov.im)

Accommodation at the observatory is basic self-catering, and you will need to take all the food, drink, clothing and equipment you need – plus a little extra as a contingency in case a change in the weather causes a delay in the return trip to the Isle of Man. Bed linen and a minimum number of blankets are provided, but in colder months a sleeping bag is advisable.

When visiting the Calf of Man, you are respectfully requested to abide by the Calf Code in order to protect wildlife and resources of the observatory and its staff.

For further information contact Manx National Heritage or see www.gov.im/mnh/heritage/countryside

BALLAUGH CURRAGH AND THE WILDLIFE PARK

In Manx Gaelic, the word 'curragh' refers to willow scrub habitat. But the area around the Curraghs Wildlife Park is much richer than willow scrub alone, consisting of a complex mosaic of inter-related peatland habitats which include bog pools, wet woodland, man-made ditch systems and fen grassland.

It's a mix which attracts a great diversity of breeding birds – and in some years, western Europe's largest winter roost of hen harriers – and supports a wide variety of plants. In summer, hay meadows spring to life with thousands of flowering orchids.

In the past, curragh was much more extensive, stretching from Ballaugh to Ramsey; isolated patches are still referred to as the Sulby or Lezayre curragh. The Ballaugh curragh adjacent to the Wildlife Park forms an area designated not only as an SSSI (Site of Special Scientific Interest) but also as a site of international importance for wetland wildlife under the Ramsar Convention. Part of the Wildlife Park itself is included in the latter.

Running through the area is a nature trail, interpretive signs along the way explaining the ecology, and as you progress you can learn how woodland has developed from open water and how, over the centuries, people have made use of the land here.

The birch woodland has grown up on hay meadows abandoned when agricultural machinery replaced the earlier horse-drawn reapers. The birch are self-sown from hedgerow trees, and the biggest and oldest are nearest the end of the trail. Where the soil is drier, bramble and ivy carpet the floor of the wood, providing shelter and feeding areas for small birds and other animals. At night hedgehogs are active and moths visit the honeysuckle flowers. In this part of the trail you can see robins, willow warblers and wrens.

Meadows are an artificial interruption of natural succession. As elsewhere, the

Orchids: an annual attraction for visitors to Close Sartfield, the flagship nature reserve of Manx Wildlife Trust.

Haymaking: cutting is done towards the end of summer, or later, to allow wild flowers to drop their seeds.

grasslands of the curragh may have resulted from the clearing of original woodland cover or – more likely – they developed from the earlier marsh vegetation of the bog stage, and regular grazing and mowing would have been enough to kill woody shrubs and to promote the growth of grasses and herbs.

Curragh habitat develops on open bog as trees take root in the drier raised clumps of vegetation. The poor conditions mean that the trees grow slowly, but when they eventually meet overhead and the canopy closes, flowers and plants which are more adapted to shade grow on the ground. As fallen branches and leaves decay, soil is built up. Gradually, the ground dries out and other species of trees are able to grow.

Willows are important to insect life, which in turn provides food for small birds such as blue and great tits, and the flocks of long-tailed tits seen in winter. The flowers and plants on the wood floor also attract insects, among them orange-tip and green-

veined white butterflies. Plants of particular interest include two or three species of orchids and the royal fern. Royal fern is unusual because the spores develop on separate spikes instead of on the underside of the fronds. It is now rare in many parts of England because it was over-collected in Victorian times for planting in gardens and conservatories.

Peat bogs can actually grow upwards, accumulating dead plant material beneath them. This doesn't decay because the acid water prevents bacteria from breaking it down and so it becomes peat. The main builder of raised peat bogs are sphagnum mosses. These absorb water like a sponge and so have the ability to grow above the water table. The presence of sphagnum here shows that the bog is still growing, but the young trees indicate that perhaps it is beginning to dry out and slow down. Trees will assist this by using up more water as they grow, thus beginning the inevitable progress towards curragh woodland. In the more open areas cotton-grass, twayblade and ragged robin flower in midsummer, but the presence of deeper-rooted and earlier-flowering bog bean shows that the water is not very far down. Surprisingly, lizards can sometimes be seen in this part, basking on the boardwalk.

Within the bog are small pools of various sizes. They are fascinating places, usually with quite different plants and animals: broad-leaved pond weed, bog pimpernel, bog asphodel and insect-eating sundew. Diving beetles live in the water and dragonflies visit and can sometimes be seen sunning themselves on the path. Growing in the deeper pools, such as once occurred in the curragh, may be the specialised bladderwort, another insect-eating plant. Common in the surroundings of all pools in this area is the characteristic wetland plant purple loosestrife.

A pool is the last remaining evidence that this area was once open water. On a small scale it shows the fate of the flooded peat diggings which we know once covered large areas in the curragh and also, perhaps, the much larger post-ice age Lake Andreas. This has already developed a bog-bean root mat over much of the surface, creating the opportunity for further changes into a bog. Bog-bean can send side shoots out and so grow over an open pool, eventually covering it completely. The shallow waters are not very attractive to ducks and provide no home for aquatic plants. This is in contrast to the original flooded peat diggings which were used by wildfowlers for many decades and which once supported such characteristic wild flowers as bladderwort.

Wildlife you can see from the nature trail hide includes mallards, geese and herons. The observation tower also gives sightings of songbirds such as finches and tits, and perhaps a sparrowhawk hoping to make a meal of one or the other. Ravens are often seen here too, since they nest on the hillside opposite the Wildlife Park. And if you're

really lucky you could even spot a hen harrier. They're a rare sight though, despite the fact that on occasion the Ballaugh Curragh contains one of western Europe's largest winter roosts of this species.

If insects are your particular wildlife interest, you could well be rewarded with sightings of damselflies and dragonflies, hawking for their prey over the pools or basking on a twig or other elevated position. Spotted orchids are common in June and include a spike or two of northern marsh orchid, recognisable by its deep purple colour. Later, yellow flag can be seen and autumn brings the development of the seed heads of typha, commonly (though wrongly) called bulrush.

This wealth of wildlife is a direct result of the area's complex history. The repeated local advance and retreat of an ice sheet towards the end of the last ice age created a lake basin between the edge of the ice sheet and the Manx hills to the south. Fine clay was deposited in the basin, leading ever since to waterlogged conditions and the classic hydrosere transition from open water to bog and fen, transformed by drainage into agricultural land in the drier parts and abandoned to nature in the wetter parts.

Up until the 19th century, curragh was an important component of the local agricultural economy. In those times, farms in the north on the sandy lands of the Jurby and Bride moraines were too dry in summer to support livestock, so they grazed instead on the Manx hills to the south. In spring and autumn, however, they grazed on the curragh land which these farms maintained, returning to the crofts to winter indoors. For generations these meadows passed down the family line and, by comparing the average size of the fields with those further north on Isle of Man walkers' maps, which show field boundaries, it is still possible to see how they were divided and redivided.

In the absence of stone, field boundaries

Sulby Glen. In the past, curragh extended as far as Ramsey, and isolated patches are still referred to as Sulby curragh.

in the curragh were constructed of soil. These provided a drier habitat for plants such as hard and buckler fern, which can now be used to trace the course of the old hedges. Ditches would have been maintained by regular clearing, ensuring a good run-off of water. The ditch banks are another specialised habitat, supporting plants such as devil's bit scabious, which can tolerate periodical clearing of the ditches and re-emerge from the seed bank in the soil.

When mechanisation arrived on Manx farms, the curragh fields ceased to be a useful part of the agricultural economy. By the early 1930s the Manx government was experimentally growing New Zealand flax in the area but abandoned the idea when war ensued. After the war, few local farmers opted to have their land cleared, and even today New Zealand flax is a surprising and exotic local addition to the area's flora. Early watercolour paintings identify many meadows which at this time reverted to scrub, and eventually to birch woodland,

with only the drier meadows on the higher land abutting the hills to the south remaining utilised.

Peat for fuel was cut from the curragh from an early date. Drainage operations must have been well advanced to permit such digging and ditching – a yearly task using a gripthang, a local type of fork with long bent tynes. The peat would have been very wet and had to be patted into cake shapes with a faayl (turf spade). The Manx Museum has photographs of peat diggings in the area, and the hills seen in the background help to pinpoint the locality.

Clues proving that this area once had many peat diggings are still to be seen on the ground – long narrow banks separating muddy pools which are more or less rectangular. Many parts of the curragh were cut for peat, mostly for burning at home, although some place names, such as the Bishop's Turbary (a field outside the Wildlife Park), imply that the Lords had various rights in the area, and peat from this plot would have been taken to Bishopscourt, a

Swathes of yellow bog asphodel – one of the very specialised plants which grow in acid bogs.

few miles away. Peat digging has also revealed evidence of an earlier history, in the shape of many pieces of bog oak and even bones of giant deer.

CURRAGHS WILDLIFE PARK

Today, other types of deer and more exotic animals can be seen in the Wildlife Park. Given the wetland setting, it's no surprise or coincidence that the Park's collection focuses on wetland species. There are, for example, three species of otter, exhibited in separate areas rather than together, as the Park is laid out on a geographical basis.

Large walk-through enclosures each contain animals from the same part of the world, and the centre of the Park is set aside for Close Beg – a children's play area with popular animals such as meerkats – and Life on Islands, where a series of linked enclosures explain how particular wildlife species arrive on islands and how evolution and human interference affect their fate thereafter.

Many islands around the world were, like the Isle of Man, connected to a mainland when sea levels were lower, and plants and animals arrived by simple colonisation. But for the largely volcanic oceanic islands, plants and animals are more restricted, arriving by drifting and gradually evolving in isolation. However, nearly all islands have been severely modified by people, and wildlife is threatened by loss of habitat. This is showcased in the Park, where Life on Islands presents three species of lemurs plus Rodrigues fruit bats, Cuban hutia, Meller's duck, Madagascar teal and the stunning Bali starling. The Park's ring-tailed lemurs are displayed separately though – on a small island adjacent to the African Bush enclosure, reflecting the nature of their island home of Madagascar in the Indian Ocean, offshore from East Africa. Other African Bush species you will see include sitatunga antelope, grivet monkey, marsh mongoose and the stately-crowned crane. Next on this wildlife tour is the European Marsh – another very distinctive wetland habitat with otters, beavers, owls, waldrapp ibis and lynx. The European beavers are uncommon in wildlife collections and in fact are part of the back-up population for the current reintroduction trial in Scotland. Nocturnal, they are rarely seen by visitors but their industry in building their lodge and cutting up the branches supplied by the keepers has to be admired.

Moving on through the Park, you come to the Australian Outback – home to red-necked and parma wallabies, along with birds such as the galah, zebra finch and white ibis. Parma wallabies are small and delicate, long feared extinct in their New South Wales home. A population was subsequently discovered on an island in Auckland harbour in New Zealand, to which they had been introduced by a Governor who had previously been Governor of New South Wales. From here, zoos around the world have acquired

animals but the surprising twist in the tale is that the parma wallaby has since been confirmed as still alive and well in the wild near Sydney.

The Park's North American trail has racoons and Canadian otters and leads to the cafe and the Amazon area. South America is the only continent with two separate exhibits – for the tropical and temperate areas – and exhibited around the Lakeside Cafe are several tropical species. Three separate islands house black-faced spider monkeys, red-handed tamarins and Bolivian squirrel monkeys, while capybara – relatives of guinea pigs and as big as dogs – wander at will around the enclosure and, in summer, can often be seen swimming in the lake. Other species exhibited here include spectacled owls, blue and gold macaws and king vultures.

Next in the Park's circumnavigation of the world is the Asian Swamp, which separates the Amazon from the Pampas and is home to red pandas, fishing cats, crab-eating macaques, short-clawed otters and a

The Wildlife Park's Chilean flamingos are native to Patagonia.

In addition to the Wildlife Park's wallabies, a population of escapees lives in the wild, mainly in the Ballaugh Curragh area.

variety of waterfowl. The Pampas enclosure is the most complete of the Park's zoogeographic assemblages in that it is possible to imagine that all the species present could be seen in one view if you were visiting Patagonia. Guanaco, mara, ruddy-headed geese, burrowing owl and Chilean flamingo are all found in this part of the world while Humboldt penguins are at home on the Pacific coast of southern South America.

The tour of the Curraghs Wildlife Park is thus complete – but there's one other surprise in store. Creatures of the night create a lot of interest, particularly when the nocturnal wildlife in question are bats. Bat boxes have been erected for some years and one, on the entrance building, is regularly used for a few weeks each spring and autumn. The droppings identify the occupant as a Natterer's bat, and pipistrelles and Daubenton's bats are also known to frequent the site, hawking for insects through the trees and over the ponds and meadows. Early risers attending the annual

Dawn Chorus event are usually rewarded with a sight of the bats as they finish their night feeding and head back to their roosts for the day.

LAND MAMMALS

For wildlife watchers visiting the Isle of Man for the first time, the mammal population presents an unusual picture. The mix of species is the result of both geographic isolation and human impact over centuries past.

So, for example, many species considered common to other parts of the British Isles are missing from the Manx countryside, yet others – far more exotic in origin – are present.

Historically, the big event that set the Isle of Man apart was the opening of the Irish Sea in the immediate post-glacial period. This created an uncrossable barrier for the migration of many species, notably moles, badgers and deer. The only archaeological evidence of the latter's existence on the island has come from skeletal remains of the

Giant Deer (Megaloceros giganteus), believed to have roamed the Isle of Man approximately 12,000 years ago.

For other absent species, such as the fox, polecat and squirrel, there is no archaeological evidence at all to support their existence here. Foxes have on occasion been introduced as quarry for other species but in all cases have been captured.

Polecats, though, present a different picture. Sightings throughout the Isle of Man are reported on a regular basis – but they are not true polecats. They are in fact a feral population of polecat ferrets, believed to originate from a number of captive ferrets released in the 1600s. Visually, it is extremely hard to tell the difference between a true polecat and a polecat ferret – especially as they are such a timid and elusive species – yet skull dimensions and DNA analysis of road fatalities have shown that their true origin is from captive populations of domesticated animals. Having escaped into the wild, the number of original animals has steadily grown and they are distributed right across the mainland area of the Isle of Man. Aggressive and successful hunters, they have exploited the niche of top mammalian predator and are often to blame for the loss of wildfowl and game birds in the Manx countryside.

The only species of the mustelid family that is both native to the island and still to be found in the wild is the stoat. Neither weasel nor otter have been recorded, other than captive specimens at the Wildlife Park in Ballaugh. Despite their native status, stoats are low in number and recent studies indicate they may be in decline in the face of competition from the polecat ferrets. Small populations are known to exist in both the north and south, but with recorded numbers falling steadily in recent years there is increasing concern for their future as a wild species.

The island is home to three species of lagomorphs (rabbit family). Rabbits are common throughout the Isle of Man, often causing extensive damage to arable crops, particularly on the northern plain. But on the higher ground they are less numerous, and in both territories bouts of myxomatosis cause frequent localised population crashes. Good numbers of brown hare live throughout lowland areas, and as a species it has fared extremely well in comparison with its cousins in lowland England, where populations have dropped drastically over the past three decades. Its success on the Isle of Man is attributed mainly to suitability of habitat and the less intensive system of agriculture.

Originally, both the brown hare and the rabbit were not native to the Isle of Man – neither reached the island in the post-glacial period before the Irish sea formed – and both were introduced by man as a source of food. Rabbits arrived in the medieval period, brought in by monks, but brown hares arrived earlier, believed to have been introduced during the Roman occupation of Britain.

In contrast, the slightly smaller and rounder mountain hare was a true native of the island, migrating northward over the frozen Irish Sea basin as the ice sheets retreated following the last Devensian glacial period 12,000 years ago. With winter-white coats they would have been well adapted in that period for life on the Manx uplands. But at some point in history, probably as a result of over-hunting, they were wiped out. End of story? No: in the 1960s a population was re-introduced to the island, and the mountain hare has successfully re-established itself in the hill ranges north of the central valley. Depending on climatic conditions, population numbers vary year on year, but as the island now gets very few days of snow cover each winter, hares can often be seen in the areas of Sartfell and North Barrule, their white coats (which develop from November through to March) easily marking them out against the dark green and purple of the upland heather.

Another introduced species – and one of the most idiosyncratic of mammals present in the north of the island – is the red-necked wallaby. Originating from the temperate maritime forest areas of Australia, wallabies have been kept as part of the animal collection at the Wildlife Park in Ballaugh since the 1960s. Individual animals have escaped from the park and colonised the adjoining Ballaugh Curragh woodland area, and over the past 40 years the feral population has steadily increased, estimated in 2011 to be between 80 and 120 animals living in the wild. Most of these feral wallabies are still located in and around the Ballaugh Curragh area, and a quiet early morning or evening walk can reward you with views of them feeding on the open grassland or stripping bark from the trees, as they do in winter months. Effectively they have occupied the vacant niche of medium-sized woodland dwelling herbivore, occupied elsewhere in the British Isles by small deer, and are exploiting the network of small fields and woodlands around the island. In recent years their increasing numbers have resulted in a wider distribution, with sightings reported from much of the north of the island, and one in 2010 from as far south as Fleshwick Bay near Port Erin.

Another unusual feral resident of the Isle of Man is the European mountain goat, found in the east of the island and particularly in the area from Laxey to Dhoon Glen. As with red-necked wallabies, their presence here is the result of animals escaping from a domestic herd, farmed in the Lonan area. They are extremely well adapted to the coastal strip's mountainous terrain, and their numbers have grown steadily to the current population of nearly 200. They often congregate in herds of 30-50 animals, and are a regular visual treat for walkers on the lower footpaths of Dhoon Glen, and for passengers travelling on the Manx Electric Railway between Laxey and Ramsey. The railway line provides the goats with an easy route along the coastal strip.

The picture changes yet again on the diminutive Calf of Man in the south, barely half a mile away from the main island across the Sound. Only three species of terrestrial mammal inhabit the Calf – the common rabbit, brown rat and the pygmy shrew. In the 1990s a colony of wood mice was recorded, but attempts to find them in the summer of 2011 failed, and it seems probable that they have died out. The Calf rabbits are notable in one particular respect – the high frequency of black rabbits amongst their numbers, believed to be the result of the escape and interbreeding with the wild population of domestic black rabbits kept by the lighthouse keepers here in the mid 1800s. Consequently, the frequency of black rabbits is disproportionately high, and they are affectionately referred to by some locals as 'Vicars' – reincarnated souls of members of the clergy.

The common brown rat is found throughout and with no predators to fear it scavenges for food very successfully, and often in daylight hours. Although originally absent from the Calf of Man, it was accidentally introduced from shipwrecks, resulting in devastation for the Calf's ground-nesting seabird population. A programme of targeted baiting aims to eradicate the rats from the Calf within the next 5 years, and their numbers are now very low. The black rat, or ship rat, has not been recorded here since 1924.

The Isle of Man supports only two indigenous species of mice – the common (and more populous) house mouse and the wood mouse, and both are well distributed throughout. Peculiarly, though, neither the field vole nor the water vole are to be found on the island, an anomaly that is unexplained given the wide distribution and ability of the field vole to survive elsewhere in more northerly regions of Europe.

Isle of Man cabbage – a wild flower confined to sandy shores and now growing only in the north.

Similarly, the common shrew is absent from the Isle of Man, as it is from Ireland. Yet its cousin the pygmy shrew does live and survive on the island. Weighing only 4 grams (less than a quarter of an ounce), this tiny mammal is a fearless little carnivore, feeding on a variety of insects and other invertebrates hunted down amongst leaf litter and undergrowth. Although active both day and night, and distributed throughout most of the island, the pygmy shrew is extremely hard to spot.

Another species for which there is no post-glacial archaeological evidence supporting its existence on the Isle of Man is the hedgehog. Yet at some point in history it has been introduced to the island by mankind and has settled into the ecosystem quite happily. Charismatic nocturnal hunters of invertebrates, hedgehogs are found in the gardens and parks of the island's suburban and urban areas, as well as in the wider countryside, and at present their population is holding steady. One particular peculiarity

is that the hedgehog flea, normally found hiding in the animal's spines, is absent from all specimens recorded to date. It's also an unfortunate fact that the most frequent public sighting of hedgehogs are those which have become road casualties – particularly in autumn, when the clocks change and peak vehicle movements shift an hour into the evening twilight.

When it comes to bat species, the Isle of Man is richly endowed, given its modest size. Of the 17 recorded species which breed in the UK, 7 are found on the Isle of Man. This is due to diversity of habitat, relatively low population density and the profusion of small rivers and streams draining from the uplands to the coast – a combination of foraging areas ideal for these animals. The nature of the landscape also provides plenty of perfect roosting sites in the form of caves, mature trees and stone buildings, many of the latter derelict.

Both species of pipistrelle bat are relatively common throughout the Isle of Man, especially in the suburban areas of the main towns, where there is no shortage of ideal roost sites. Even in the most urban areas, they can be seen hunting around rooftops. Almost as common as the pipistrelle is the delightful brown long-eared bat. This can often be detected flying around the edges and tops of trees, and among hedgerows and small woods, and it prefers to roost in old buildings.

Largest of all the Manx bat species is the Leisler's – at least twice the size of the pipistrelle and a high flyer, swooping over linear features such as rivers, roads and hedgerows, and picking off the larger flying invertebrates. Most easily found in the west, it emerges in early dusk. In stark contrast is the Daubenton's bat – a low-level acrobat which sweeps over water, often just a few centimetres above the surface, and picks off the emerging freshwater invertebrates. It roost in trees and old man-made structures, such as bridges and tunnels, often close to the water.

Relatively scarce around the island is the Natterer bat, but rarest of all the Manx species is the whiskered bat. Slightly larger than the pipistrelle, in summer months this furry bat dwells in the crevices of houses and buildings. Pregnant females get together to form a maternity roost, but in winter and cooler months they often prefer caves.

The best places to observe bats tend to be wooded areas lying near or alongside rivers – sites which provide the ideal combinations of foraging territory for a variety of species. In the west, well-known 'batting' locations include Glen Wyllin, Glenfaber Bridge and The Raggart; in the north, Pooyldooey; in the south, Monks Bridge at Ballasalla; and in the west, Summerhill Glen and along the old Douglas to Peel railway line.

AMPHIBIANS AND REPTILES

Only two species of amphibian and reptile are truly native to the Isle of Man, although a few non-native species have been found here in the past.

The only true native amphibian is the common frog, found in ponds and wetlands throughout the lowland areas and especially in the central valley, the northern plain and in and around farms and rural properties throughout the south of the island.

A phenomenon regularly reported is that the frog tadpoles are very slow or late to develop, as seen most frequently in ponds, winter wet scrapes and ditches at the higher elevations, where winter and spring temperatures and a shortage of food are the main reasons for this delay. Many of the open ponds in the heather uplands have a higher acidity level and do not support frogs, and the variable flow rates and water levels of most streams and rivers do not support them either. However, the wet meadows, ditches and woodlands lying alongside these rivers and streams are often good places to find frogs.

In recent years non-native amphibians have been introduced into the Manx countryside. Most notable are the common or smooth newt and the palmate newt, found in many ponds in the areas of Douglas, Onchan and northwards to Baldrine. Escapees from populations held in domestic garden ponds, they have successfully colonised many garden and farm ponds in the eastern parts of the island – but to the detriment of the native frog population, as both species of newt can feed on frog tadpoles.

Surprisingly to many, the common lizard (*Lacerta vivipera*) is also a true native of the Isle of Man. Relatively small, it is the only member of the reptile group to survive here, due to the fact that it gives birth to live young – an adaptation (known as viviperisation) which gives rise to the Latin name for the species and which allows it to colonise and reproduce in areas that are much cooler than those demanded for survival by most other reptiles. As a result, common lizards can be found scattered

Common spotted orchid – abundant at Close Sartfield in late spring and early summer.

throughout much of the lowland areas of the Isle of Man, and even at some quite high elevations – up to around 1,000 feet (300 m) above sea level.

Throughout the Manx countryside, the abundance of stone outcrops, man-made stone walls and earthen banks provides these animals with a wide variety of spaces and voids for refuge and over-wintering hibernation. Where these sites occur on the south faces of slopes or walls, with much-needed warmth and sunshine for basking and tall grass or herbs for hunting for food, the conditions for these animals to make their homes are optimum. On the island's north-western shores, the combination of sandy beaches, dunes, marram grass, gorse and heather banks similarly provides conditions favourable to their survival.

By walking quietly, and keeping a careful watch in suitable basking spots, there is every chance of spotting one of these delightful creatures in the right areas. Good locations for seeing common lizards are at the Ayres in the north, along the Ballaugh shoreline in the west and around the cliffs in Port Erin Bay in the south. Keen-eyed observers can also see them on Douglas and Onchan headlands. And travellers resting for a pint, or watching the bike races at the Creg ny Baa on the TT course, can be lucky enough to spot them in the nearby walls.

Non-native reptile species are absent from the Isle of Man. An occasional individual specimen of grass snake or slow worm has been recorded in the past – an escapee, or released from captivity – but the combination of relatively low average summer temperatures, high rainfall and often cold winters has prevented any from surviving in the wilds of the Manx countryside.

INVERTEBRATES

As is true of other places in the British Isles, the extent of knowledge about the Isle of Man's animal inhabitants is defined by the experts available to find and name them – and this applies especially to invertebrates (animals without backbones, or 'mini-beasts').

Some groups of invertebrates are better understood than others, such as butterflies (described elsewhere in this guide) and moths, but others have scarcely been studied at all. And although the full picture of the Isle of Man's invertebrate wildlife has yet to emerge, we do know that the island has fewer species of most groups than does the UK. The reasons for this are the island's small size, its temperate and often damp climate, and its isolation from mainland Britain since shortly after the end of the last ice age. On the other hand, the Isle of Man packs a surprising variety of habitats into such a modest area, and the wildlife hot spots offer plenty of scope for visiting naturalists with a particular interest in invertebrates.

THE AYRES AND NORTHERN SANDY COAST

Without doubt, one of the most exciting places for insect life on the Isle of Man is the Ayres National Nature Reserve (NNR) on the north coast. The dune system and associated heath support a variety of specialist species able to cope with the exposed, dry conditions. Many thrive in the warmth generated quickly by the sun in the well-drained ground, and such conditions support some insects which otherwise would not survive on the Isle of Man.

Amongst the most intriguing are the burrowing solitary bees and wasps which can be seen flying to and fro between their breeding burrows and the sources of food collected to provision underground nests for their offspring. One of these species is *Colletes succinctus*, a small brown burrowing bee which collects pollen and stores it underground for its larva. An important pollinator, *Colletes* also unwittingly provides a home for one of the Isle of Man's specialities – the heath bee-fly (*Bombylius minor*). As its name suggests, this intriguing little furry fly resembles a bee and has a long forward-pointing proboscis with which it probes flowers for nectar. Its larvae live inside burrowing bee nests, stealing the food stores laid down by the unfortunate parent bee and even eating the rightful occupant. The female beefly has the extraordinary habit of flicking her eggs into the bee burrow while hovering outside the entrance. Apart from the Ayres, the only other sites in the British Isles for this Red Data Book species are on the Dorset heaths – so its presence on the Isle of Man has a special significance, and it is duly protected from collecting or disturbance by the island's Wildlife Act. The adult flies can be seen on the wing in July and August.

Another characteristic solitary bee of the Ayres is the leafcutter bee (*Megachile maritima*) which, like a number of other insect species, is here on or near the northern edge of its range in the British Isles because of the favourable localised conditions. Like garden leafcutters which make their unwanted impression on roses, *Megachile maritima* snips chunks out of leaves with which to line its nest in a burrow in the sand.

Fairly common amongst the Ayres solitary wasp species is *Ancistrocerus scoticus* – one of the potter or mason wasps (Eumenidae) which construct clay-lined cells inside cavities such as hollow plant stems. A parasitoid species, it catches and paralyses with its sting other invertebrates such as caterpillars, and stores them in the brood cell for its hatching larva to eat. It is an attractive little wasp, marked black and yellow, and if you are interested in hymenoptera behaviour it is worth looking out for on a sunny day.

The Ayres coast is home to many other invertebrates confined to its warm soils and sheltering dunes. There is space in these pages to mention but a few, one of the most

important species from a conservation management point of view being the Red Data Book (Endangered) moth called the scarce crimson and gold (*Pyrausta sanguinalis*). A pretty little moth, protected by Isle of Man law, it flies during the day amongst the ground-hugging vegetation for just a few weeks in high summer. Its larval food plant is wild thyme. Other moths which specialise in the Ayres upper shore and dune habitats include the sand dart (*Agrotis ripae*), shore wainscot (*Mythimna littoralis*) and Portland moth (*Actebia praecox*).

One striking Ayres inhabitant to look out for, wandering over herbs and shrubs, is the red and black bug *Corizus hyoscyami*. This species belongs to the Heteroptera, a group of insects with mouthparts formed into a proboscis which is used to suck plant juices or the body fluids of invertebrate prey. *C.hyoscyami* is yet another species whose presence on the Isle of Man puts it on the northern edge of its British Isles range.

Many other of the north coast's invertebrates are ground dwellers, either burrowing into the sandy soil or sheltering amongst the dune plants or under stones. The large ground beetle (*Broscus cephalotes*) lurks under stones and driftwood and preys on sandhoppers. Amongst the spiders, the wolf spiders (Lycosidae) and Ozyptila crab spiders (Thomisidae) are characteristic ground dwellers and include the superbly camouflaged hunter *Arctosa perita*.

Around the coast to the west of the Ayres is Manx Wildlife Trust's Cronk y Bing nature reserve. The tall marram grass is ideal for the large funnel-shaped webs of the spider *Agelena labyrinthica* and the nursery webs for newly-hatched spiderlings of the wolf spider (*Pisaura mirabilis*). Even the strandline and roots of plants colonising the head of the beach are home to some specialist terrestrial invertebrates. The woodlice *Armadillidium pulchellum* and *A.album* have both been recorded along these shores. Sand dune snails include the pointed snail (*Cochlicella acuta*), 15-20 mm long.

The low cliffs of the north-west and north-east coasts are part of the thick blanket of glacial sediment covering the island's northern plain. In addition to the variability of drainage, the animals that live here must be adapted to a substrate which is prone to instability and erosion by the sea. There is still much to learn about the invertebrate communities of these cliffs, but one species which has been well studied has a particular significance for natural history in the Isle of Man – Cowin's robber-fly (*Machimus cowini*).

This grey-brown, long-legged bristly fly of the family Asilidae was discovered near Douglas in the 1930s by a Manxman, Will Cowin, after whom the species was named. It has since been recorded in the Ballaugh Curragh area and in neighbouring countries along Irish Sea coasts, but its current Manx stronghold appears to be the soft cliffs between Ramsey and the Point of Ayre.

Robber-flies are fairly easy to observe, but there are several species, including *M.cowini*, which are very similar to each other and can only be reliably told apart by entomologists with some experience of the group.

OTHER COASTAL HOT SPOTS

Depending on the time of year, invertebrates you can expect to see around the island's mostly rocky coast will be those associated with the flower-rich coastal grassland and heather-covered cliff tops.

At the Sound, a low south-facing cliff eroded into the glacial sediment covering the bedrock is home to burrowing bees which, although solitary in their nest-building habits, tend to aggregate. They are often harassed by wasp-like cuckoo bees of the genus *Nomada*, which lay their eggs in the burrowers' nest so that their larvae can eat the food intended for the rightful occupants. Here at the same time in late spring/early summer are green tiger beetles (*Cicindela campestris*), fierce little predators with jewel-

The soft cliffs of the north-east coast – a favoured habitat of Cowin's robber-fly.

Lady's smock in a typical garey (wet pasture).

like bright green metallic colouring. Very active during the day, they are fast runners and flyers. Their larvae live in open burrows in the ground and if anything they are even more voracious than the adults, their formidable jaws seizing anything that moves across the burrow entrance. Another characteristic beetle, considerably slower-moving than the tiger beetle, is the minotaur beetle (*Typhaeus typhoeus*), 20 mm long, black and heavily built. One of the 'dor' or dung beetles, it buries rabbit dung for its larvae to eat and is common around the Sound and on the Calf of Man. The male has two long forward-pointing 'horns' on the thorax, giving the species its English name and making it easily recognisable.

A spectacular and rewarding walk for wildlife watchers is Marine Drive, a section of road (closed to motorised traffic) along the cliffs south of Douglas. Butterflies and other insects visit the wild flowers growing on the rock faces, and the mottled

grasshopper (*Myrmeleotettix maculata*) frequents the springy turf on the cliff tops.

In the south, a walk along the spectacular cliff tops of Spanish Head takes you through heath dominated by heather and western gorse, alive with the hum of bumblebees. Keep an eye open and amongst the heather you could see the cocoons of the emperor moth (*Saturnia pavonia*). In spring the day-flying males of this distinctive species are searching for females with which to mate. Later in the autumn, you may encounter hairy caterpillars of the fox moth (*Macrothylacia rubi*) wandering across the coastal path in search of a hibernation or pupation site. The larva of this moth is a host for the parasitic grub *Tachina grossa*, the adult of which looks like a very large and hairy black house fly with a yellow head. You can't really mistake the very distinctive adults as they visit flowers of hogweed or wild carrot.

Amongst the coastal rocks lives the inconspicuous thrift clearwing (*Synansphecia muscaeformis*). More like a fly than a moth, the larvae of this species feed in the roots and stems of thrift. Until recently the species was thought to be rare on the Isle of Man, but the increasing use of artificial pheromone to attract the male moths has helped to establish that it is more common and widespread than previously supposed. Other notable Manx moths along the coast include the lichen-feeding dew moth (*Setina irrorella*), the pod-lover *Hadena perplexa ssp. capsophila*, the black-banded *Polymixis xanthomista ssp. statices* and the grey *hadena caesia ssp. mananii*. This last species, whose larvae feed on the seed pods and leaves of sea campion, is protected by Isle of Man law. Male dew moths fly in the afternoon and evening, but the other species are best detected at light traps or by searching for larvae with a torch.

A well-known hot spot for wildlife is the Langness and Derbyhaven Area of Special Scientific Interest. Accessible by public footpath, its reputation as a key birdwatching location is built on the abundance of invertebrate food, especially on the beaches and in the salt marsh. Many thousands of sandhoppers, beetles and fly larvae, including those of the spotty-eyed hoverfly (*Eristalinus aeneus*), live in the rotting seaweed and other organic debris that builds up on the strandline, providing a feast for birds such as choughs, starlings and wagtails. But Langness is perhaps best known amongst entomologists for the lesser mottled grasshopper (*Stenobothrus stigmaticus*) – the only known location in the British Isles where it can be found. At just 10-15mm long, this unassuming little grasshopper inhabits the heathery grassland and is fully protected by Isle of Man law.

Coastal habitats are also home to the island's only two species of bush crickets, which appear to be confined to just a few sites here. The dark bush cricket (*Pholidoptera griseoaptera*) inhabits the blackthorn and brambles along the steep coastal slopes above

Laxey Bay, while the speckled bush cricket (*Leptophyes punctatissima*) was until recently known only from Perwick Glen and beach to the west of Port St Mary. Its discovery in Glen Maye on the west coast in 2009 was something of a surprise and left the island's naturalists puzzling over how this flightless insect came to be in a location 14 kilometres to the north.

WOODLAND, PLANTATIONS AND UPLAND

By medieval times, the Isle of Man was largely deforested and the remnants of its ancient woodland banished to inaccessible cliffs and ravines. For this reason, the island is not rich in woodland invertebrate species and is devoid, for instance, of native longhorn beetles. However, there are some invertebrates which are fairly typical of the steep-sided wooded glens, which in the Victorian era were planted with trees and used as pleasure gardens.

Glen Maye, an Area of Special Scientific Interest showing vestiges of ancient woodland habitat, is home to moths such as the swallow-tailed (*Ourapteryx sambucaria*), phoenix (*Eulithis prunata*), coxcomb prominent (*Ptilodon capucina*) and cloaked carpet (*Euphyia biangulata*). A walk through the more flowery parts of the Isle of Man's coniferous plantations may reward you (if you're observant) with a sighting of some specialist hoverflies. The bumblebee mimic (*Eriozona syrphoides*) can be seen feeding on purple flowers such as knapweed whilst its larvae are predating aphids on the conifer trees. Another hoverfly to look out for is *Xylota jakutorum*, which has a liking for buttercups. A largish fly, it has a long, parallel-sided abdomen which in the male has paired orange spots. The more common hoverflies can also be quite abundant in these flower-rich areas.

One welcome recent sighting in Dhoon Glen was of a rhinoceros beetle (*Sinodendron cylindricum*), the larvae of which tunnel into

Spring squill at Port Grenaugh, west of Santon Head on the south-east coast.

rotting hardwood. Another deadwood borer, but of conifers, is the wood wasp (*Urocerus gigas*). The large yellow and black female, with its formidable-looking ovipositor, appears quite intimidating but is harmless to humans. The larvae are attacked by the large parasitic ichneumon wasp (*Rhyssa persuasoria*), which has a very long and scary-looking whip-like ovipositor used to 'inject' an egg down between the wood fibres and into the hapless host's tunnel.

As farmland and plantation give way to upland moor and acid grassland, the invertebrates you might expect to meet are similar to those of windswept coastal heaths, particularly where heather and bilberry survive sheep grazing. However, you might be lucky enough to find the mountain or bilberry bumble bee (*Bombus monticola*), a declining species in the British Isles, or – around a moorland pool – the sombre-coloured black darter dragonfly (*Sympetrum danae*).

FARMLAND AND WAYSIDE

Exploring the Isle of Man's lowlands takes you through a patchwork of small fields bounded by dry stone walls or by the characteristic 'sod hedges' – banks topped with turf and gorse. Scrubby field corners and hedges along quiet lanes can be rewarding for wildlife watchers. In spring, the flowering blackthorn and hawthorn attract many insects, and autumn-flowering ivy is a crucial end-of-season food source for hoverflies, wasps and bees. Where livestock is grazing nearby, you might expect to see the hoverfly *Rhingia campestris*, distinctive for its forward-pointing 'snout', and the larvae of which live in cow dung.

Amongst the flowers and berries you may spot shield bugs – relatively large, slow-moving and easy to observe. Commonly seen are the hawthorn shield bug (*Acanthosoma haemorrhoidale*), the predatory brown and spiky *Picromerus bidens* and occasionally the purple-brown and greenish

Traditional Manx sod hedges, such as these at Sandygate (north-west), are a haven for wildlife, particularly wild flowers.

sloe shield bug (*Dolycoris baccarum*). Larger still, and often encountered in early summer, is the cockchafer beetle or Maybug (*Melolontha melolontha*), sometimes a pest in gardens or agricultural crops but otherwise completely harmless, though noisy and clumsy.

FRESHWATER AND WETLAND HABITATS

Reservoirs and fire pools in Manx government plantations are attractive to wildlife. Particularly accessible (with due care) are Clypse and Kerrowdhoo Reservoirs near Douglas, Cringle Reservoir south-west of Foxdale, the fire pool in South Barrule Plantation, and the privately-owned Ballannette nature reserve near Baldrine. Depending on the time of year, most of the island's dragonfly and damselfly species can be observed at these locations. Common hawker (*Aeshna juncea*), common darter (*Sympetrum striolatum*), common blue damselfly (*Enallagma cyathigerum*), blue-tailed damselfly (*Ischnura elegans*) and large red damselfly (*Pyrrhosoma nymphula*) will almost certainly be there, and at South Barrule fire pool the black darter (*Sympetrum danae*) also occurs. Less commonly, the emerald damselfly (*Lestes sponsa*) may be found and, in early autumn, the occasional migrant hawker (*Aeshna mixta*).

Smaller reservoirs and dubs (ponds), especially on the northern plain, are home to some distinctive water beetles and bugs, though few of the sites are open to the public. Species recorded relatively recently for the first time include the green great diving beetle (*Dytiscus circumflexus*) and the cherrystone beetle (*Hyphydrus ovatus*). Amongst the water bugs, the water scorpion (*Nepa cineraria*) and water cricket (*Velia caprai*) are readily identifiable. Freshwater snails include a bladder snail (*Physa fontinalis*), great ram's-horn snail (*Planorbarius corneus*), several wandering pond snails *Lymnaea* and tiny orb mussels *Pisidium*.

Isle of Man rivers and streams are generally modest in scale compared with river systems in mainland UK and Ireland, and are fast flowing for most of their length. Since they do not pass through major industrial conurbations, they are reasonably unpolluted and support stoneflies and mayflies associated with well-oxygenated water.

The most extensive and important area of Isle of Man wetland is the Ballaugh Curragh – an Area of Special Scientific Interest and an internationally-recognised Ramsar Site, to the north of the Wildlife Park. A new inventory of its invertebrate fauna is long overdue, and most recent records have concentrated on the butterflies, dragonflies and damselflies, all of which are common in other parts of the island. Nevertheless, amongst the more obvious insects will be *Donacia* or reed beetles, which come in a variety of colours – metallic bronze, purple or green – and clamber about in the tall wetland vegetation. Their larvae live in the underwater parts of marsh and aquatic plants. In the more open areas and marshy grassland you are likely to find (or hear) common green grasshoppers (*Omocestus viridulus*).

MAN-MADE HABITATS

The Isle of Man's rich mining heritage has provided habitats for animals that would otherwise live in caves. Accessible to the public, the mine adit above Laxey Wheel is home to the cave spider (*Meta menardi*), which suspends teardrop-shaped silken egg sacs from the walls and ceiling. Elsewhere, cool damp cellars and outbuildings suit the daddy-long-legs spider (*Pholcus phalangioides*).

Stone walls provide ideal homes for invertebrates that prefer crevices and small holes. In recent years, several small colonies of the red mason bee (*Osmia rufa*) have been found burrowing into mortar in stonework. Spiders also take up residence where there

Ragged robin, perfectly at home in a buttercup meadow.

are crevices. *Segestria senoculata* lays a characteristic series of 'trip wires' radiating out from the entrance to its hole. Similarly, bluish tangly silk clinging to stonework marks the lairs of *Amaurobius* spiders.

Parks and gardens attract not only the usual insect visitors but also, occasionally, exotic migrants such as the hummingbird hawkmoth (*Macroglossum stellatum*), which hovers at flowers and probes for nectar with its long proboscis.

WILD FLOWERS AND THEIR HABITATS

Rightly so, the Isle of Man is renowned for its wild flowers. Through spring and summer they coat the hills, glens, meadows, verges and coast in a delicate pastel patchwork of colour.

About 500 species of wild flower are native to the Isle of Man. That is to say, they grow here naturally, alongside 1,000 or so other wild flower species which over thousands of years have been introduced to

the island by humankind. And although they are all attractive, it is the native wild flowers which are of most interest to conservation, because these are the species which support most of the island's wildlife.

The term 'wild flowers' doesn't just mean the likes of daisies and primroses but ferns, trees and grasses too. Most native species are directly descended from the first wild flowers that colonised the island after the last ice age more than 10.000 years ago, when rising sea levels separated the Isle of Man from Great Britain and Ireland.

WHERE WILD FLOWERS GROW

There are various factors which influence where wild flowers will grow. Geology, for example, determines the type of soil, and on the Isle of Man the geology is dominated by acid slate, which means that acid-tolerating plants such as heathers flourish.

A small area of limestone around Castletown gives rise to alkaline soils, and in turn to some of the island's most fertile soils.

Flowering Manx heath.

The northern plain is dominated by deep glacial soils which arrived when massive glaciers from the north melted to leave behind their cargo of trapped stones (often from Scottish mountains), sand and silt.

Then there's the climate – dominated by the Gulf Stream, bringing warm water from the tropics to Isle of Man shores and a considerable amount of rain to Manx hills. In winter, temperatures are higher than the British average but conversely cooler in summer. The interaction of climate and geology concentrates rainfall on to hilly places and leaves areas such as the northern plain relatively dry and sunny.

There's also a third determining factor – mankind, who arrived here about 5,000 years ago, discovering an island blanketed in forest, with perhaps just the tops of a few hills bare and a few open marshes. We know this from pollen preserved in peat that shows a dominance of oak, hazel, alder, birch, willow, pine and elm trees, with very little grass pollen. When agriculture arrived on the island, the position rapidly changed, with a dramatic reversal and increase in grass pollen. This fast conversion from forest to agricultural created the traditional cultural landscape we have today.

THE UPLANDS

In many places the original forested uplands would have been on a deep fertile soil, but light and well drained so that it would have been easier to work with the basic Stone Age and Bronze Age tools of the day. A less dense forest would also be easier to clear or to graze out by domesticated stock. But, unfortunately, the island's heavy rainfall gradually washed away the fertile soils and, along with a cooling of the climate, made the ground unfit for most agriculture. By the end of the Bronze Age, all that remained was an open heath landscape. Over the next few thousand years, woodland periodically re-colonised.

The upland landscape that dominates about a third of the Isle of Man today is similar to that left to us by our prehistoric ancestors, with great swathes of flowering heath interspersed with rocky outcrops, boggy mires and drifts of cotton-grass. It's ironic that this large area of biodiversity-rich habitat was created by a human-made prehistoric farming catastrophe, but the open hills are now one of the gems of the island's wildlife. Today, all open uplands are managed by a combination of grazing sheep and controlled burning of heather in winter. The upland heaths are a habitat which, globally, is confined to the extreme north-west of Europe and, furthermore, has its own special biodiversity – thus the Isle of Man is obliged and committed to exercising sensitive management of these uplands.

So what of the hill tops that were never covered in forest? Even today, Snaefell is home to one species found nowhere else on the Isle of Man – the least willow (*Salix herbacea*). This extremely low-growing Arctic/alpine bush barely grows above the stones and gravel in which it stands, and is so small that even experienced ecologists have difficulty finding it. The best way to spot it is to look for the little catkins in spring.

WOODLAND

Just a few hundred years ago the Isle of Man was considered by visitors to be a barren, treeless place, except for a few tiny woodlands which, for two reasons, survived millennia of woodland clearance: one, they grew in steep, sheltered ravines and two, there was still a local need for the wood they produced.

Although there is very little historical evidence to support the existence of this woodland, and how it was managed, there is plenty of ecological evidence. This is in the form of species that rarely grow away from woodlands and do not re-colonise new woodlands when they appear. So where several of these plants grow together, it supports the proposition that it's indicative

of a continuity of woodland cover. Such plants are known as ancient woodland indicators, and examples which include the locally-rare wood speedwell and wood sedge can still be found in sites such as Dhoon Glen, Glen Maye and Groudle Glen, to which there is free public access as each is a designated National Glen.

Some of the Isle of Man's best woodland can be seen in these National Glens. As well as relic fragments of the native woodland, they also contain fine specimens from Victorian tree planting, growing in fern-draped valleys. Indeed, in the past few years, woodland species such as woodpeckers and speckled wood butterflies have taken advantage of this mature woodland by colonising. However, most of the broadleaved woodland is not planted but spreading naturally.

In the past century and a half, woodland has seeded itself along many of the Isle of Man's rivers and streams and become established in wetlands and along field boundaries. There is more native woodland now than there has been for hundreds – if not thousands – of years, and the process of woodland expansion continues today. Bluebells, wild garlic and many species of fern rapidly colonise these woodlands, giving them an ancient natural feel.

Of all the island's woodlands, the most noticeable are the plantations. King's Forest on Greeba Mountain was planted by the Manx Government in 1906 – the first of many conifer plantations that eventually covered about 3.5% of the landscape. In 2000, planting stopped to protect the upland heath. The last vestiges of the initial 1906 planting still exist as stunted Scots pine and larch high on Greeba Mountain. More than 100 years on, they are draped in lichen growth and look much like a natural Scottish pine forest. While the plantations are not generally considered a boon to nature, the young spruce trees are favoured by nesting birds and the plantation tracks

provide space for sheltered heathland glades as well as recreational opportunities for thousands of people.

WETLANDS

Wetlands as a description of wildlife habitat includes rivers, ponds, marshes, bogs and reservoirs. In fact, wetlands are the Isle of Man's most important habitat group, supporting over a third of the native wild flowers.

Most visitors to the island's countryside tend to see only a few ponds – known locally as 'dubs' – though more than 350 exist, mostly hidden in farm fields in the north. These dubs cover just the tiniest fraction of the Isle of Man but contain a huge number of wetland plants, such as waterlily, pennyroyal and the strangely-named triffid-bur marigold. And although not widely seen or known about, dubs are crucially important to the island's biodiversity, containing more rare species than any other habitat.

Up in the Manx hills are reservoirs,

created to provide drinking water. The largest is Sulby, opened in 1982 so not yet old enough to have an abundance of wild flowers. But the older Injebreck Reservoir is more developed and supports rare plants such as corn mint, growing on exposed banks as water levels drop in summer, and masses of shoreweed – a native waterweed which provides shelter for wildlife that in turn feeds the trout so prized by fishermen. Other smaller reservoirs, such as Cringle and Clypse, are surrounded by accessible wildlife-rich habitat, with orchids and other wild flowers growing in abundance.

The bogs and mires which exist in the hills are a completely different kind of wetland, composed of saturated peat, and looking like dry land – until you venture on to them. They are fearsomely inhospitable habitats for wildlife, with virtually no fertility, soil almost as acid as vinegar, and a cold, wet climate with a short growing season. So the plants which *do* manage to grow here are specialised, and often beautiful – from the delicate cotton-grass to the

Least willow in flower on the slopes of Snaefell.

Spring sandwort flowering in May on a 'dead' – the old copper mine on Bradda Head, Port Erin.

splendid bog asphodel and the carnivorous sundew, the latter catching insects in its sticky leaves to supplement its diet. Rare species also occur here, the most spectacular being cranberry, which can transform an area of bog into a display of pink flowers and red berries. And from an environmental point of view, these bogs – which continue to grow and accumulate peat – lock away more carbon and so help in the battle against climate change.

The Isle of Man is well known for its famous 'curragh' (pronounced currack) – a Manx Gaelic term for an area of lowland bog or lots of willow scrub, although traditionally completely treeless. This is in contrast to the term 'garey', which refers to a marshy field normally full of rush. There are many areas of curragh on the island but the main one is the Ballaugh Curragh (often known simply as the Curragh). Even today it is wild and not frequently visited, but well worth seeing for its wild primeval appeal, twisted trunks of lichen-encrusted willow

lying over still, stagnant water, and a feast of wildlife on view.

Its flora is a diverse mix of wetland plants. Stunning royal ferns grow six feet high or more. Twayblade orchids impress with their green flowers, and bog-bean with its flamboyant white blooms. Just a hundred years ago the site was an open marsh, where local people came to cut peat for fuel, and the willows that grow now invaded soon after the area was abandoned and left unmanaged. The few remaining open glades still retain some of their original flora, such as the scented bog myrtle bushes and purple loosestrife.

The best of the other curragh sites is the Central Valley, between Peel and Douglas, and it can be seen from the Heritage Trail – a walk along the disused railway line that once connected the two towns. In many parts the woodland here is much older than that of the Ballaugh Curragh, and the woodland vegetation is much more developed – larger alder trees, big tussock

Maidenhair fern growing on cliffs close to Glen Maye.

sedges and swathes of marsh marigold. So although smaller than the Ballaugh Curragh, from a biodiversity perspective it is every bit its equal.

Marsh (or garey as it is known locally) can easily be picked out as fields colonised by rush. They tend to be full of wild flowers, though as most are permanently grazed they rarely get a chance to flower well. When they do, look out for meadow buttercups, ragged robin, lady's smock and meadowsweet.

MEADOWS

A meadow is defined simply as an area of grassland cut for hay. On the Isle of Man the tradition is to cut after Tynwald Day (the national day of celebration, held usually on 5th July) and then graze the grassland with sheep or cattle during autumn and leave it to grow again in spring. By removing the hay every year, the fertility of the site is reduced, allowing less competitive wild

flowers to colonise alongside the grasses. If a site is managed for many years, more and more wild flower species will colonise it.

Flowering meadows put on a somewhat short-lived show from the end of May to the beginning of July, but if you catch them they are stunning. They have survived well on the Isle of Man and there are still a few hundred acres, scattered around the countryside. The best are on the fringes of the Ballaugh Curragh, where the Curragh bog gives way to more solid if slightly damp and acid soils. This is the perfect place to see wild orchids, with hundreds of thousands on view at the best site, Close Sartfield – a Manx Wildlife Trust Nature Reserve and one of the finest meadows in the British Isles.

Every year paths are cut through the meadows and you can explore at your leisure or, during Orchid Week (the second week in June), join one of the regular guided tours.

THE COAST

From open beaches to sea cliffs to sand dunes, the Isle of Man coastline is remarkable for its wildlife and wild flowers. About one in five of the native plant species is either dependent upon, or mostly found within, the coastal habitats.

Sand dunes are located mainly around the north coast, and particularly at the Ayres. You will also find a few dunes on the south coast, near Castletown, and before the days of Victorian concrete promenades there were dunes at Douglas, Peel and Port Erin.

The dunes are covered in tall marram grass, once used for thatching roofs, and in amongst it are species such as sea holly, sea bindweed and the rare Isle of Man cabbage. In July the dunes are coloured by bright purple pyramidal orchids. At the tide line, specially-adapted plants such as prickly saltwort and sea sandwort grow and start to collect sand around their roots, gradually forming new 'embryo' dunes. Dunes are the island's natural sea defences, growing seawards a few inches or more every year as sand eroded from cliffs is carried along on air currents. In smaller bays and beaches, sand is replaced by shingle storm beaches, the shingle supporting deep-rooting plants such as sea kale, sea beet and sea radish.

In areas sheltered from the worst of the waves, plants can become established below the high-tide mark, creating salt marshes. The plants that grow in these conditions are very specialised, able to survive several hours under the sea every day. Sea aster, samphire and sea purslane are a few of the species that form a saltmarsh, and unlike many other habitats new native species are free to colonise the island as their seeds drift in the current from all over the Irish Sea, so species such as sea lavenders and cord grasses appear from time to time. The best saltmarshes are at Langness and Poyldvaaish on the south coast, but Cornaa (near Maughold on the east coast) and Ramsey harbour (east coast) also have significant areas.

The rocky coast is where the best wild flower displays occur, May being the best

Sea kale in a lovely location, overlooking Port St Mary.

A typical meadow of the flat northern uplands (near Jurby in the north-west).

month. Pink drifts of thrift are abundant all over the coast, growing with sea campion, bucks-horn plantain, kidney vetch, bird's-foot trefoil and many others. Later in the year, daisy-like sea mayweed comes into flower and its leaves can be rubbed gently to reveal a scent of camomile. As the cliffs get steeper and less accessible, rarer plants grow, such as hay-scented buckler fern, royal fern and a plant more familiar as a house plant – the delicate maidenhair fern. They all grow where fresh water trickles over the rocks and meets the humidity and warmth of the sea. Just above the high-tide line, small brackish pools and marshes often occur, displaying unspectacular but often rare and unusual grasses and sedges.

MINE DEADS

Thousands of years of mining for copper and lead on the Isle of Man means that there are areas where mine spoil has been dumped, rendering them extremely toxic. Known locally as 'deads', these areas show that remarkably, every niche is soon occupied, either by species that have long evolved to be tolerant of these conditions or species that have more recently evolved tolerant strains.

On Bradda Head, near Port Erin, the tiny spring sandwort grows on an old copper mine, flowering every May with cushions of white star-like blooms. Cross-vein Mines to the north-west of South Barrule is notable for its bizarre ferns, moonwort and adder's tongue that in summer grow out of the lead-mine spoil. These ferns only grow an inch or two here, but often in their hundreds. The lead spoil also contains calcite, a rock rich in calcium carbonate, making the spoil very alkaline and enabling flowers such as common centaury and fairy flax to occur in an abundance not normally seen in the uplands.

Northern marsh orchids on sand dunes on the north-west coast.

Sundew – a specialised plant supported by peaty soils.

WILD FLOWER CONSERVATION ON THE ISLE OF MAN

When it comes to protecting biodiversity, the size of the Isle of Man is a disadvantage. The smaller the area, the fewer the opportunities a species will have to find suitable safe habitats. Manx native wild flowers are a good example. In Great Britain, wild flower loss over the last 200 years has been 13 species out of 1500, whereas the Isle of Man has lost over 40 out of 500 – more than ten times the extinction rate. Although this is not an indication that the Isle of Man has done anything wrong particularly, it does show that an extra-special effort will be necessary in future to ensure that further loss of wild flower species is minimised.

The key to the future of saving rare wild flower species is ensuring that the remaining habitats are well maintained under traditional management methods. This means action such as opening up farm ponds again to allow cattle to wallow in them and eat out invasive reeds and willows. In woodlands, reintroducing 'coppice management' – a traditional technique for woodland management, not practiced on the Isle of Man for generations – would produce a perfect habitat for wild flowers, songbirds and some insects.

Small, targeted actions often produce long-term sustainable solutions for biodiversity loss – and indeed these are gradually being implemented.

Druidale, on the south-western tip of Sulby Reservoir,
is a natural paradise for man and for wildlife.

WILDLIFE IN RIVERS AND STREAMS

Most of the Isle of Man's watercourses are fast-flowing flashy streams, the major exception being the sluggish Lhen Trench – a man-made channel created several centuries ago to drain the original wetlands of the low-lying northern plain. Although pollution from the defunct mining industry still affects a few streams, the relatively low intensity of agriculture and lack of heavy industry means that overall the island's water quality compares favourably with that of the UK.

Despite their modest size, the rivers and streams provide food and habitat for a wide variety of native species. As woodland is scarce, riparian trees and shrubs also provide important habitat corridors for many wholly terrestrial creatures.

FISH

Three types of salmonid fish are native to Manx watercourses. Brown trout (*Salmo trutta*) are resident all year round and can be found in surprisingly small streams, while sea trout, their migratory form, start returning from the sea as early as June, depending on rainfall. Atlantic salmon (*Salmo salar*) tend to start running up river from late September and are mostly what are known as grilse, having spent only one winter at sea. Non-

Atlantic salmon

Cock salmon

native rainbow trout (*Oncorhynchus mykiss*) are stocked in several of the Isle of Man's reservoirs for recreational angling, and escapees are occasionally spotted in running waters.

Although trout and salmon tend to be held up as the flagship species, two other fish have attracted increasing attention in recent years. European eels (*Anguilla Anguilla*) spend most of their lives in still and/or running freshwaters before returning to the Sargasso Sea to spawn. Unfortunately, populations across their range appear to have reduced drastically since the late 1970s and are now regarded as outside safe biological limits. Various reasons for their demise have been proposed, including over-exploitation by commercial fisheries, infection by swimbladder parasites, and alterations in ocean currents reducing juvenile recruitment to rivers. Research conducted since 2007 indicates that the Isle of Man has a relatively healthy population, probably due to the absence of a commercial eel fishery. Although they can grow to over a metre, European eels can be difficult to spot, often encountered only when they are migrating across damp fields. .

Lampreys are among the most primitive of all living vertebrates and are not, strictly speaking, true fish. Until recently the last recorded sighting of a lamprey on the Isle of

Man was in 1981, in the Sulby River. It is likely that, as elsewhere, they suffered badly from pollution in the lower reaches of rivers during the 19th and early 20th centuries. In addition, their migration would have been – and may remain – restricted by the building of weirs. However, since 2007, brook lamprey (*Lampetra planeri*) have been found in the rivers Dhoo, Neb and Sulby, river lamprey (*L. fluviatilis*) in the River Neb, and further unidentifiable *Lampetra* specimens have been observed in the River Glass and the Llen Trench. Research to determine more about their distribution on the Isle of Man is ongoing.

The other native fish of Manx watercourses are the minnow (*Phoxinus phoxinus*) and the three-spined stickleback (*Gasterosteus aculeatus*). The ten-spined stickleback (*Pungitius pungitius*) has been found in some ponds and may be present in sluggish streams such as the Lhen Trench. Coarse fish are not native and, while a few species are present through introduction in some ponds and reservoirs, they are rarely encountered in watercourses.

INVERTEBRATES

While some river invertebrates such as aquatic worms, water mites and flatworms are permanent residents, many of the more familiar – mayfly, stonefly and caddisfly

Brook lampreys, River Sulby.

nymphs, for example – are the juvenile stages of terrestrial insects and an important food source for fish. They are also useful as a means of monitoring water quality. As species vary in their tolerance of environmental factors, including pollutants, the invertebrate community of a watercourse can give a better indication of its general health than can chemical analysis of a water sample.

OTHER WILDLIFE

Grey wagtails nest in and near river banks and can often be seen hopping between stream boulders in their search for insects. Reaches which flow more slowly are often inhabited by wildfowl such as mallards, mute swans, geese and moorhens, especially where bankside vegetation is dense enough to provide suitable nesting areas. The Silverburn at Castletown and further upstream by Rushen Abbey are particularly popular places to 'feed the ducks', as the feathered residents make obvious to people passing by!

One of the Isle of Man's most spectacular birds, the grey heron, is often seen hunting for fish and eels along the stream banks and shallows. Kingfishers are occasional visitors to the island and most often seen on the Lower Sulby, but are not known to breed here. And on summer evenings look out for Daubenton's bats, hunting for insects on or near the surface of stiller reaches. One of seven bat species native to the Isle of Man, they often use old stone bridges as roosting sites.

WHERE TO ENJOY MANX RIVERS

The Forestry Directorate of DEFA (Department of Environment, Food and Agriculture) manages a number of National Glens, many originally developed for the Victorian tourist trade, where you have free access to enjoy the beauty and wildlife of many of the island's streams and rivers. Several other sections of publicly-accessible paths also border watercourses.

Waterfowl on the River Sulby.

Ballaglass Glen in Maughold, south of Ramsey, is managed as a semi-natural woodland. The mix of tree species consists of a central core of mature oak with magnificent mature beech on the glen's eastern and southern edges. South of the Cornaa River, the woodland is mainly mature larch and pine, and around the old mine buildings is an area of natural regeneration of willow, birch and ash. Access to Ballaglass Glen is by car, bus or the Manx Electric Railway, and it is very popular with artists and photographers.

Bishopscourt Glen lies on the A3, just north of Kirk Michael on the TT course. A narrow glen of about 5 hectares, it stretches for around half a mile towards the hills and is planted with mixed hardwoods and shrubs. The glen was formerly part of the private garden belonging to the Bishops of Sodor and Man, who resided at Bishop's Court opposite the glen's entrance. Access is by car or bus, with reasonable wheelchair access too.

Colby Glen is in the village of Colby, near the main A7 road. The Colby River runs through the glen with footpaths on either side, and the glen is particularly attractive for its mature broadleaved trees, the main species being beech, elm, sycamore and ash. During spring and early summer, wild bluebells and primroses bloom in profusion. Access to the glen is by car, bus or the Isle of Man Steam Railway, the station at which to alight being Colby Halt.

Dhoon Glen is 5 miles south of Ramsey, on the A2 Douglas to Ramsey coast road. With its splendid waterfalls and great natural beauty, it has long been a favourite for photographers. It is one of the Isle of Man's steepest glens, descending for over half a mile through a wooded valley to the shore. The main path follows an old cart road and meanders through a dense canopy of trees. Ash, witch-elm and alder dominate, with significant numbers of sycamore, birch and rowan also present. Half way down the valley is the spectacular waterfall known as

West Baldwin Reservoir.

the Inneen Vooar or Big Girl, and it drops more than 40 metres (130 feet) in two stages. Access to Dhoon Glen is by Manx Electric Railway, bus or car.

But perhaps the best known of the Manx glens is **Glen Helen** in the west, north of Ballacraine on the TT course. Created by a consortium of Manx businessmen interested in arboriculture, it opened to the public in 1867. Today you can see a great variety of mature and impressive trees, including sequoia, thuja, spruces, Douglas fir, oak, sycamore and beech. Paths traverse the glen alongside the rivers Neb and Blaber, and three quarters of a mile into the glen is the picturesque Rhenass waterfall. Glen Helen also has a children's play area and toilets, and refreshments are available from either the nearby hotel or restaurant. The glen has ample parking and reasonable access (plus toilet facilities) for disabled visitors. You can get to the glen by car or bus.

The River Neb can also be enjoyed along a walk of about a mile and a half, from the harbour at Peel. It is one of the Isle of Man's best salmon and sea trout rivers and in 2006, in the area known as the Raggat, a dilapidated weir was replaced by a rock ramp (about a mile from the harbour). This aids their upstream migration, the low-flow channel not only allowing fish of many different sizes to pass through but also creating a greater variety of flow conditions than is possible with a traditional weir.

On the coast road south of Peel is **Glen Maye**, or Glen Mea (once known as 'The Luxuriant Glen'). About 11 acres in size, it straddles either side of the Rushen River and boasts a magnificent waterfall. The glen's beautiful and sheltered fern-filled woodland includes relics of the ancient forests that once covered the Isle of Man. Apart from several fine Monterey pines at the top of the glen, the majority of the trees are ash, sycamore and elm. Glen Maye also supports plants which are not found anywhere else on the Isle of Man, such as wood vetch, hairy brome and the 'Glen Maye bramble' –

a 'micro-species' variant of the common blackberry (*Rubus fruticosus agg.*). The beauty of the glen owes much to the spectacular abundance and diversity of attractive ferns such as hart's tongue, soft shield fern, polypody, lady fern, hard fern and broad buckler-fern, all of which abound in the mild, sheltered climate. At its lower end, before reaching a pebbled beach, the path passes towering cliffs where fulmars nest and you can sometimes see other seabirds, and hawks. You can get to Glen Maye by car or bus, but many prefer to use the coastal footpath (Raad ny Foillan – Road of the Gull) from Peel or Port Erin.

A mile south of Kirk Michael on the west coast is **Glen Mooar**. It occupies part of the western bank of the Glen Mooar valley and extends southwards from the main Peel to Kirk Michael road to the small coniferous plantation beyond the spellbinding Spooyt Vane (White Spout) waterfall – one of the island's highest. Although it stands outside the glen's boundary, visitors are welcome to view it courtesy of the owner, Mr. T.J. Curphey. Like Glen Maye, you can get to Glen Mooar along the Road of the Gull coastal footpath (from Peel or Port Erin), or by car or bus.

Just south of Kirk Michael on the coast road from Peel lies **Glen Wyllin**. From a trickle in midsummer to a torrent when in full spate, the stream follows the course of the glen to the sea. In previous times the stream has powered a water mill, hence the name ('Wyllin' being Manx Gaelic for 'mill'). With a children's playground and a busy campsite, operated by the local Commissioners, the glen is popular in summer, and in the upper half, along its southern side, are mature woodlands. Two stone towers rise in the glen's mid section – remnants of the Manx Northern Line railway – and lower down, past the waterfall, is a grassy paddock popular for picnicking. Access through Glen Wyllin by car or bus is easy, the road travelling its full length

Silverburn near Rhen Abbey.

leading to a car park by the sandy shore, and wheelchair access is easy too.

Two miles north of Douglas, on the coast road to Laxey, is **Groudle Glen**. The upper section contains excellent specimens of beech, though in the lower section pine and larch are more abundant. An unusual feature of the glen is a small waterwheel and pump house, used originally to pump water up to the Groudle Hotel. Further down the glen is the narrow gauge passenger-carrying Groudle Glen Railway, operated on various days throughout the year by local enthusiasts, the line turning around the headland to a small cove. Access to Groudle Glen is easy – by car, Manx Electric Railway or on foot from Onchan or Douglas.

Between Douglas and Ramsey on the main A2 road is **Laxey Glen**. Here you are treated to a rich variety of mature exotic trees, as well as areas of more naturalistic woodland.

There's also a restaurant, café, play area and grass paddock, hence its popularity with families, and access to the glen is by car, bus or Manx Electric Railway.

Running parallel to the quietly-flowing Groudle River is **Molly Quirk's Glen** –

small, narrow, well-wooded and bounded at each end by a road bridge. According to legend, Molly Quirk was a local woman, robbed and murdered here, but there is no evidence or bad vibes to substantiate such a tale.

At the lower end of the glen, the eastern boundary is marked by the 'Whitebridge', under which a boarded walkway enables you to continue into Groudle Glen, and adjoining Molly Quirk's is another short but pleasant streamside pathway known as Bibaloe Walk. You can get to Molly Quirk's Glen by car, bus or on foot from Onchan.

Three miles south of Douglas, in rolling countryside close to the Old Castletown Road, is **Port Soderick Glen** –15 acres, through which runs the Crogga River. The natural attractions here include conifers and spring bluebells, and a marshy area on the southern side is populated with 'Blughtyn' (marsh marigolds). In 2006 an additional 30 species of Manx wild flowers were introduced into the central meadow. From a practical viewpoint, Port Soderick Glen offers the added advantages of onsite parking, wheelchair access along some of the pathways, and the fact that you can get to it by bus or Isle of Man Steam Railway. Also very popular is the easy but spectacular coastal walk along Marine Drive which takes you south from Douglas Head to Port Soderick.

Close to the Isle of Man's Ronaldsway Airport, and next to the village of Ballasalla in the south, is **Silverdale Glen**. Currently, the family attractions here include a café, restaurant, shops and boating lake, together with a children's playground featuring a unique Victorian water-powered roundabout. To the north is a large grassy paddock. Getting to Silverdale is very easy – by car, bus or on foot from Ballasalla Station, on the Isle of Man Steam Railway. Furthermore, much of the glen and the area it occupies has wheelchair access.

Another attraction of Silverdale is that

most of the Silverburn River can be followed from nearby Castletown on the south coast, up to about a mile above where Silverdale Glen ends at the A3. Less than a mile upstream of Castletown harbour the channel contains a large stepped weir, immediately above which you can see a good example of 'green' riverbank engineering. To prevent the river diverting from the weir, this tight bend had previously been reinforced with stone held back by steel mesh which eventually failed, leaving a bare, vertical and rapidly-eroding bank. In 2006 a softer approach was employed, using hazel faggots, coir roll and geotextile laid over the newly-profiled bank, which was subsequently planted with trees such as willow and alder and marginal plant species such as flag iris, canary reed-grass and common reed. The benefits were numerous: not only more aesthetically pleasing and wildlife-friendly, but energy from the water flow was absorbed by the faggots, coir roll and marginal plants. The pool on this bend is now a good place to observe brown trout, and salmon and sea trout rest here on their upstream migration.

In a different setting altogether is **Tholt-y-Will Glen**, close to Sulby Reservoir and lying in the shadow of Snaefell – at 2,036 feet the Isle of Man's highest point. With steep sides, Tholt-y-Will nestles in the upper reaches of Sulby Glen (also known as **Glen Mooar**), one of the most scenic areas of the entire Manx landscape. The glen descends in winding paths alongside a mountain stream, tumbling over rocks and forming a tributary of the Sulby River – the longest of the Isle of Man's rivers. Although not easily accessible by public transport, there is ample parking space near the glen's lower entrance.

In the island's south-east is the Santon Burn. It contains no National Glens but is partly accessible by footpath and, relatively speaking, is unusual compared with other examples of larger Manx rivers in that it has not been subject to extensive canalisation in its lower reaches. Consequently, it meanders naturally through substantial sections of its length and in 2009 the construction of a fish pass alongside a major weir (not publicly accessible) reopened several miles of excellent river habitat to the salmon and sea trout that run its course.

HELP TO CONSERVE MANX RIVERS AND STREAMS

These simple guidelines are intended for residents and visitors, as appropriate.
● Dispose of litter and other waste correctly, and seek advice from DEFA if garden waste contains invasive plants such as Japanese knotweed.
● Make sure that washing machines and similar devices are plumbed in correctly.
● Report suspected pollution or poaching activity as soon as possible.
● If you own or tenant land with a watercourse, be aware of your rights and responsibilities.
● Seek advice and approval before commencing any works in a stream or along banks.
● Store grass cuttings and compost heaps at least 10m from the banks of streams.
● In spring and summer, check stream banks for any signs of invasion by Japanese knotweed, Himalayan balsam and/or giant hogweed, and seek expert advice on control methods.
● Conserve water. The less that's consumed, the more there is for Manx rivers.

USEFUL CONTACT NUMBERS

● General enquiries, DEFA: 01624 685835
● Fisheries Directorate, DEFA: 01624 685857
● Flood Risk Management Team, IoM WSA: 01624 695949
● To report pollution: 01624 685885
● To report poaching: 01624 685857

THE WORK OF DEFA: THE DEPARTMENT OF ENVIRONMENT, FOOD AND AGRICULTURE

DEFA monitors water quality, provides advice on river management and pollution prevention, and also investigates pollution incidents, taking legal action where necessary.

The Fisheries Directorate of DEFA is responsible for the supervision, protection and development of freshwater fisheries, including monitoring salmonid populations and conducting anti-poaching patrols.

The Flood Risk Management Team of the IoM Water & Sewerage Authority (IoMWSA) is responsible for the maintenance (in relation to flood risk) of legally-designated 'main rivers', and issues consents for works likely to affect any watercourses on the Isle of Man. Although concerned primarily with flood management and prevention, it increasingly uses wildlife-friendly methods when repairing river banks and weirs.

As elsewhere in the British Isles, Manx rivers have been subject to anthropogenic impacts which can be detrimental to their ecology, including obstructions to fish passage, flow regulation, invasive plants, and the typical legacies of historic drainage schemes (such as straightened, over-widened and/or deepened channels). The Isle of Man Government seeks, where possible, to address these issues through a combination of direct action and providing advice for landowners and tenants.

FREE INFORMATION LEAFLET

The *Manx Watercourse Management Guide* is available by download from www.gov.im or by request from the Fisheries Directorate, DEFA.

Hen harrier – most easily seen between September and March from the Manx Wildlife Trust's reserve hide in the Ballaugh Curragh.

WILDLIFE ON THE WING

WHERE TO WATCH BIRDS

Arguably, the main focus of attention for birdwatching on the Isle of Man has to be the coast, whether it's the sheer cliffs and rocky shores of the south or the long, sandy, pebbly beaches of the north. But there are many attractions inland too. The hills are mostly rounded in outline, traversed by excellent roads and easily explored by car and on foot, and the wooded glens are very scenic and rich in bird life. The larger reservoirs are disappointing though, only Kerrowdhoo attracting a modest variety of wildfowl.

Largely rural in nature, the Isle of Man promises you rewarding birdwatching wherever you go. But, of course, there are hot spots – locations where experience shows that you can expect good birding – and this guide focuses on the top nine sites.

THE AYRES: POINT OF AYRE TO THE LHEN

The Ayres is an area of coastline comprising 8 km of sand dunes, and within this is the Isle of Man's only National Nature Reserve. The Point of Ayre marks the island's most northerly point and, running west from here to the Lhen Trench, the coast on either side of Rue Point offers

Golden plover – a wader which frequents Langness in the south and the Ayres in the north.

you the best opportunity to see waders.

Flocks of oystercatcher, ringed plover, golden plover, sanderling, dunlin and curlew can reach three figures, with turnstone regularly seen. From early spring through to late summer, large numbers of gannet feed offshore in the fish-rich shallow seas. At the Point of Ayre during summer, rafts of Manx shearwater – often exceeding 1,000 – can be seen floating offshore along the entire length of the beach system, as can feeding eider and all three species of diver.

Sandwich tern pass through the area on spring and autumn migration, with some non-breeding birds staying for the summer, joined in late summer by family parties from Irish breeding sites. Small numbers of Arctic and little tern breed annually. Inland of the beach, the extensive area of dune heath supports good numbers of breeding skylark and meadow pipit. Wheatears occur on passage, and inland of the heath a variety of woodland passerines can be found in the dune slack.

Though currently closed to public access so that commercial activity and restoration work can take place, the gravel pits to the west of the road which leads to the Point of Ayre regularly produce flocks of more than 100 – wigeon, mallard, pochard, tufted duck and coot – together with smaller numbers of teal and goldeneye.

Sea-watching is most rewarding during spring and autumn, especially when the wind is from the north or west, though calm days give the best chance of seeing divers, sea duck and shearwaters offshore. The best time to see waders is 2-3 hours either side of high water.

GLASCOE DUB

In Manx, a dub is a pond and this rather unassuming example (a farm pond) is one of many scattered over the island's low northern plain. But in terms of the variety of species it attracts, and the ease with which you can view them, it is by far the best, and a very worthwhile stopping point – especially as the adjacent grazed fields are prone to seasonal flooding.

Winter flocks of wigeon and teal regularly exceed 100. Truly wild mallard are present too, as are resident domestic specimens! In some winters small flocks of whooper swan and pink-footed goose arrive. Shoveler, shelduck, gadwall, pintail and pochard are all seen on occasion. Snipe are usually present in winter, and an interesting variety of other species use the dub and flooded fields nearby, such as oystercatcher, redshank, lapwing, curlew, wood sandpiper, greenshank and common sandpiper.

And although winter offers you the best viewing opportunities, the flooded fields are increasingly producing decent birding in spring and autumn months.

BALLAUGH CURRAGH

Covering 478 acres (190 hectares), this is the Isle of Man's only designated RAMSAR site and it comprises an extensive area of

Langness, the Ayres and Glascoe Dub are all locations favoured by oystercatchers and birdwatchers.

Kittiwake is present in great numbers on the Sugar Loaf stack and adjacent cliffs (south-west), and at Maughold Head (north-east).

willow, silver birch and marshy grassland. Within this are reserves managed by Manx National Heritage (202 acre/82 ha) and the Manx Wildlife Trust (31 acres/2.6 ha). The first of these two reserves has a network of paths leading you through wet woodland, the other comprising carefully-managed hay meadows, where in spring there is a spectacular display of orchids.

A wide variety of bird species is present here at various times. Water rail, feral greylag goose and woodland species such as long-tailed tit, siskin, lesser redpoll and treecreeper are resident through the year. In spring and summer you can also see woodcock, curlew, grasshopper warbler, blackcap, willow warbler and spotted flycatcher, all of which are among the many species that breed here annually. Corncrake, shoveler and teal breed occasionally, though the latter probably more regularly than is generally thought.

In winter the site is known for its communal roost of hen harrier – at one time considered to be one of the largest in western Europe – but more recently numbers have dropped, probably as a result of the site scrubbing over (the natural succession of wetland to woodland).

If you visit between September and March, you have the best chance of watching hen harriers coming in to roost, arriving at the Manx Wildlife Trust's reserve hide at least an hour before sunset. For the highest counts, choose evenings which are windy. From the hide, you can see large flocks of greylag goose, and the squealing of water rail is almost guaranteed – plus you have a good chance of seeing other raptors such as sparrowhawk and merlin, and maybe even barn owl.

Visit in spring and you can listen for roding woodcock – again in the hours prior to dusk – but calm evenings are preferable to catch the evocative call of the curlew, the flight song of lesser redpoll and the 'reeling' call of the grasshopper warbler.

MAUGHOLD HEAD

Within the area of Maughold Head, on the Isle of Man's east coast, is one of the island's four main seabird colonies. The terrain is a mix of sheer cliffs and steep grassy slopes.

This is home to the largest cormorant colony, now holding well over 100 nests. Fulmars, shags, razorbills and black guillemots all breed along the coast here, as do a small number of puffins – a species not common to the Isle of Man – and the dominant species are kittiwake and guillemot. Several pairs of chough – a real Manx speciality - breed along this stretch of coast, and peregrine falcon and raven continue to breed annually.

PEEL

Switch your attention to the west coast and, from the northern end of Peel Bay through to Contrary Head south of the town, you'll discover an interesting assortment of maritime habitats – slate cliffs, a low rocky islet, a small sandy cove and a protected bay with a fine sandy beach. And inland is upland heath, characterised by a mix of gorse and heather but including extensive tracts of bracken too. Put it all together and you have very good opportunities for birding and for walking.

On the rocks around Peel Castle you can see wintering flocks of turnstone and purple sandpiper. In autumn, good numbers of kittiwake frequent the breakwater and fulmar are often seen scavenging off the end of it. Large groups of eider feed in the bay and around the seaward side of the breakwater and castle rocks. From early April through summer, look out for black guillemot along the coast south of Peel. Great close-up views of this species are on the cards, as recently they have taken to prospecting suitable holes in the breakwater and inner reaches of the harbour.

When sea-watching from the castle's seaward side, you could well catch sight of gannet, Manx shearwater, storm and Leach's petrel, skua and a variety of gulls and waders – all seen regularly at the right time of year. And the coast south of Peel is the best place on the Isle of Man to see puffin. Any time between mid-April and early July should prove rewarding, with the bonus of the sights, sounds and smells unique to an active seabird colony – in this case mainly kittiwake and guillemot, with shag, razorbill and fulmar hatching too for good measure. Chough, peregrine and raven also breed along this stretch of coast.

Sea-watching can be exciting any time from early summer through to late October. For best results choose a west or south-westerly wind. Purple sandpiper can be seen in most months except June to August. For breeding seabirds the period from late April to mid-July will give most reward.

EAIRY AND KIONSLIEU DAMS

In total, these two man-made dams comprise nearly 15 acres (6 hectares) of shallow fresh water and associated marginal vegetation.

Tufted duck and coot breed and are present here throughout the year, and it is likely that teal also breeds in the wet area between the two dams. In winter you can see a larger variety of wildfowl, including whooper swan, wigeon, gadwall, mallard, pintail, pochard, scaup, goldeneye and goosander. You could also see water rail, and snipe are probably present in greater numbers than is apparent to the eye.

Spring and summer will show you good numbers of sedge warbler and willow warbler, along with other songsters such as blackcap and long-tailed tit. Swallow, sand martin and house martin all feed over the dams.

Visiting the dams is worthwhile at any time of year, though winter is favoured for wildfowl and spring/summer for woodland species.

Arctic tern, which breeds in small numbers at the Ayres (north).

LANGNESS AND DERBYHAVEN

Together, the Langness peninsula and its bordering bays of Derbyhaven and Castletown add up to the Isle of Man's best birding spot. Within it are large areas of intertidal rock and sand (the island's closest equivalent to intertidal mudflats), saltmarsh, exposed coast, sheltered bays, gravel beaches, rock pools, low cliffs, grassy slopes, scrub and the short grass of a golf course – a remarkable mix of habitats. And add to this the peninsula's location, at the extreme south-east of the Isle of Man coastline, which is an irresistible draw for breeding, wintering and migrating species.

Flocks of wigeon, teal and mallard – each exceeding several hundred in number – are seen here in midwinter, and eider arrives in increasing numbers too. Well in excess of 60 shelduck are seen in early spring, several pairs staying on to breed. Other regular visitors, though in smaller numbers, are goldeneye and red-breasted merganser, and pintail, shoveler and long-tailed duck are seen from time to time. Brent goose (the pale-bellied form) occurs annually, in some years of flocks of more than 40. The island's best site for great crested, red-necked and Slavonian grebe is Derbyhaven, and the bay often plays host to great northern diver and several black guillemots, especially during or shortly after storms.

The most numerous wader species are oystercatcher, golden plover and curlew, with ringed plover, dunlin, redshank and turnstone occurring in good numbers. Smaller numbers of grey plover and a few lapwing can be seen, the latter still hanging on as a breeding species. A variety of other waders can be observed too, mainly on passage or overwintering, and these include bar-tailed and black-tailed godwit, whimbrel, greenshank, little stint and knot, with snipe wintering on the salt marsh. Little egret are now annual visitors, and in increasing numbers.

Skylark breed on the peninsula in good

numbers, as do meadow and rock pipit. Other passerines are also well represented – the likes of stonechat, linnet, reed bunting, sedge warbler and whitethroat.

In terms of species and numbers, passage migration is well represented, a large variety of rarities having been seen over the years. In addition to some of those already mentioned, the more predictable include wheatear, redstart, whinchat, grasshopper warbler and white wagtail. The beach systems of the area, particularly on the Castletown Bay side of the peninsula, provide good feeding in the autumn and winter for flocks of chough, which in some winters comprise 60 or more birds.

Whatever time of year, the Langness and Derbyhaven area is well deserving of a visit. High tides tend to produce the most rewarding birding as birds are pushed off the intertidal feeding and roosting areas into a narrow strip of exposed foreshore.

THE CHASMS AND THE SUGAR LOAF

Between Port St Mary and the Calf Sound is the Chasms – an area of deeply-fissured rock cliffs which overlook the Sugar Loaf stack and form a spectacular backdrop to the sea below. On the Sugar Loaf and adjacent cliffs, narrow horizontal ledges make ideal nest locations for thousands of kittiwake and guillemot.

A summer visit to witness this cacophony of noise and activity is highly recommended. Breeding fulmar, shag and black guillemot are here too, and the sheer cliffs provide ideal feeding and breeding opportunities for kestrel, peregrine, raven and chough. Standing on top of the cliffs, you can be rewarded with close-up views of all these latter species as they catch the updrafts and glide effortlessly past at eye level.

THE CALF OF MAN

Lying just 600 m off the extreme south-west tip of the Isle of Man is the Calf of Man, and also within this channel of water is the much smaller islet Kitterland. For birdwatchers, the Calf of Man is a vital part of the Manx story and experience, as it has been a Bird Observatory for more than 50

The Langness peninsula, a graveyard for shipping in pre-lighthouse times, is a haven for birds, many migrant visitors making landfall here.

years. It is managed by Manx National Heritage and staffed every year from March to November.

The main focus is to monitor migration and breeding success, though much good work is done too in habitat management and restoration. Annually, more than 30 species breed here, many of them seabirds and including gulls (lesser black-backed, herring and great black-backed), kittiwake, fulmar, guillemot, razorbill and black guillemot. But 'pride of place' goes of course to the Manx shearwater, at one time nesting here in countless thousands but, by around 1790, almost extinct on the Calf. In 2000 it was discovered to be breeding here again, and since then numbers have steadily increased, though the population is still a shadow of its former self. Raven, chough and peregrine breed here annually too, and hen harrier and short-eared owl do so occasionally.

It was on the Calf, in the early 1990s, that the first Manx breeding of eider occurred, and the species is now well represented here, as are stonechat, wheatear and linnet (the latter two also occurring as passage migrants), and meadow pipit, rock pipit and wren are numerous.

Migration periods are a great draw to ardent birdwatchers, and over the years the Calf of Man has documented the comings and goings of many species, some rare – amongst them mourning dove (the common dove of North America), pechora pipit and Baltimore oriole – and others more common. Examples of the latter include goldcrest and chiffchaff, some of the earliest arrivals, observed in late March/early April, followed by willow warbler and wheatear. As spring progresses, so does the migrant list, with a variety of common warblers, redstart, whinchat and spotted flycatcher occurring annually. Rarities are also eagerly anticipated every year, the likely candidates including hoopoe, red-breasted flycatcher and great reed warbler.

For some species autumn migration is a mirror image of spring, but species such as yellow-browed warbler, firecrest and a number the less common buntings and finches may be expected.

Late summer and autumn is usually the most rewarding time for sea-watching, when thousands of Manx shearwater can be seen heading south towards their wintering quarters off South America. You can also see sooty and cory's shearwater, and all of the main skua species, auks, petrels and divers.

On suitable days in summer you can take a boat trip to the Calf of Man from Port Erin, but if you're planning to stay overnight prior booking through Manx National Heritage is essential as accommodation is limited. For contact details see page 11.

BUTTERFLIES

For butterfly enthusiasts the Isle of Man presents an interesting mix of common and not-so-common species, with eighteen regularly recorded and a few migrants occasionally adding to the number. Over the past 10-20 years the dynamics of migration, coupled with climate change, have produced some interesting changes in populations and the appearance of two new species on a regular basis.

The best places to go to see butterflies are dependent on the time of year and, most critically, the availability of food, either as nectar from flowers or as the favoured food-plant for a particular species. For example, the Ayres in the far north of the island is a good location for several species, the low-lying sandy terrain attracting common blue (the larvael food plant for which, bird's-foot trefoil, is in plentiful supply), orange-tips, whites (large, small and green-veined), small tortoiseshell and dark green fritillary.

Flight period for the vast majority of species on the island is between mid-April and mid-October, with just a few specimens of some species (examples being red admiral and small tortoiseshell) occasionally seen

Painted lady, a delightful summer visitor to Manx shores.

outside this time frame. Several species have second broods, which means there can be two peaks of activity when you can spot them.

The most common species found throughout the Isle of Man is wall brown, recorded from all but the highest hills and regularly seen during its two-flight period of May/June and August/September.

Also frequently seen are large white, green-veined white, red admiral and small tortoiseshell. All four species have a similar distribution, found throughout lowland coastal areas, the central valley, the lower hills of the south and the low-lying northern plain, particularly in the area of Ballaugh Curragh. These locations reflect the distribution of favoured food plants – brassica in the case of whites, and stinging nettles for the larvae of red admiral and small tortoiseshell. Sheltered river valleys, meadows and suburban gardens give you good opportunities to observe these species.

Two other members of the whites regularly found are the orange tip and small white. Orange tip is widely distributed through most of the British Isles and has a single brood which hatches in April and May, the latter being the best time to see it on the Isle of Man. Its larval food plant, cuckoo flower (*cardamine pretensis*), prefers damp unimproved grasslands, of which there are plenty in the Manx countryside, and this species does well here and can be found in any areas of flower-rich meadow around the island. The males are highly active and easily identified by their distinctive bright orange wing tips. The females display a less active flight pattern and wing tips are a far more understated grey, with a single grey spot on the forewing.

Small white, similar in size, has a double grey-black spot to the forewing and an unmottled white or pale yellow underwing. Recorded throughout the island, small white has a distribution similar to that of several of the other whites, since its primary larval foodplants (plants of the cruciferae family) are widely distributed throughout the hedgerows, curragh woodlands and meadows.

Two species of blue butterfly can seen on the Isle of Man – common blue and holly blue. Common blue is a frequent flyer in much of the lowland areas, open grassland and lightly wooded habitats – in fact anywhere where it can find its main larval food plant, bird's-foot trefoil. Unlike in the south of England, where this species is double brooded, on the Isle of Man it has a single brood and consequently in most years is on the wing for a shorter flight period – from early May to early September. Holly blue, although recorded across much of the Isle of Man, is more localised in its distribution and is best found in the areas of the Ballaugh Curragh, the central valley (from Peel through to Douglas) and in the south, from the Port Erin area eastwards through to Castletown. The Isle of Man is at the very northern limit of the holly blue's distribution, and although double brooded (best flight periods are May and August) numbers in most years are limited and it is comparatively scarce.

Two species which are relative newcomers to the Isle of Man are comma and speckled wood. Both have colonised the island in the past 10 years, and both are on the increase. Speckled wood is fairly distinctive, with hind-wing ringlets and forewing white speckles over a dark grey-brown background and a crenulated trailing edge to the hind wing. Common throughout the majority of the British Isles, the adults favour shady woodland glades and clearings, feeding on honeydew secreted by aphids and scale insects. Unrecorded on the Isle of Man before 2006, when it was found in Port Soderick Glen, the species has steadily increased its numbers and distribution to take advantage of the available habitats, and can now be seen in most of the broadleaf woodlands and glen areas around the island. In similar vein, comma has spread from its

early recording site in the Ramsey area through the Ballaugh Curragh and down the west coast to the Peel area. You can also find it in new colonies in and around Douglas. A medium-sized butterfly with a 'ragged' appearance to the wing edges, and black markings over a golden chestnut-brown background, comma is double-brooded and the larvae feed on nettle, elm and willow, of which there is a plentiful supply in the Manx countryside. The adults' main nectar sources tend to be thistle, bramble, knapweed and privet – as well as the ubiquitous Buddleia – and consequently this species is best found in sheltered spots among scrubby woodland, and along hedgerows, gardens and old railway lines.

As a result of their habitat requirements, some Manx species are less widespread and far more restricted in their distributions. Grayling is a coastal specialist, found primarily along the Ayres shoreline and around Marine Drive, on Langness and the coastal cliffs around Port Erin and the Meayll peninsular. It has a single brood each year and the flight period is relatively short – just six to seven weeks from late June through to mid-August – and of the six subspecies of grayling found in the British Isles only one, *ssp semele*, is seen on the Isle of Man. Its larval foodplants are grasses (red fescue, sheep's fescue and marram grass all feature in its menu), and the adults tend to feed on thistles, bramble and heather.

Another habitat specialist is the dark green fritillary, which has similar coastal preferences but can also be found in some upland and curragh areas. It's a common sight on the Calf of Man and at the Ayres, but there is more chance of finding it on the island's west coast than elsewhere. Distinctive for its highly-specked black spots over an orange-brown background, this butterfly can often be seen resting in heather and feeding from thistles and knapweed in its favoured breeding areas – habitats which are well stocked with common dog violet, the caterpillars' food-plant. It is a single-brood species, and there are two subspecies in the British Isles. Only one of these – *ssp semele* – occurs on the Isle of Man and is best seen on calm sunny days in June and July.

Painted lady is one of the most distinctive migrant species seen in the British Isles, and in most years a small number make their way across the Irish Sea to reach Manx shores. A delightful summer visitor, it is similar in size and colouration to the red admiral but with a brighter orange wash colour to the hind wings and rear half of the forewings. Wintering in North Africa, painted lady migrates northwards through Spain and France each year to reach the southern shores of the UK in May. Usually, individuals arrive on Manx shores from the start of June (depending on weather and winds) and in a good year can be seen through to the end of September.

Another inhabitant of North Africa, and a migrant visitor in most years, is the clouded yellow – a species sometimes recorded over-wintering in southern Britain, but as the Isle of Man is towards the northern limit of its annual migration it does not survive here over winter. Consequently, its numbers are highly dependent on weather conditions and the size of populations elsewhere across Spain and France, and can vary from several hundred in a good year to none in a poor one. Best locations on the Isle of Man are the lowland areas just inshore of the south coast.

There are several other species for keen butterfly observers to look out for. For example, the small copper – often found in dry sunny banks during its two flight periods of late May/early June and July to September. Its larval food plant is common and sheep's sorrel.

The meadow brown (*ssp splendida*) is on the wing from June through to September. With an extensive supply of larval food plant (various grasses), and a wide variety of

nectar food plants for the adults, this species is more of a habitat generalist and is widespread throughout Isle of Man hedge banks, railway lines, sheltered glades and edges of meadows and woods.

Almost as widespread in its distribution, but far less easily observed as a result of its low-flying nature and close-wing resting posture, is the small heath butterfly – visible on the wing from May through to September. This species appears to be increasing in number, but as it is inconspicuous it has probably been previously under-recorded, and despite its name can be seen in a wide variety of habitats, as its larval food plants of bents, fescues and meadow grasses are widely distributed.

Probably the most easily and commonly-identified species is the peacock butterfly. This is found throughout much of the island – in fact, wherever there are suitable nectar sources and good availability of its larval food plant, the common nettle. Over-wintering adults are usually seen on the wing in mid-spring, from April into May. After laying their eggs on the underside of nettle leaves, they disappear until the year's new progenies emerge in August and September, and then feed and mate before going into hibernation again. Peacock butterflies are popular and frequent visitors to gardens and flower-rich meadows, where nectar sources are freely available.

Wildlife on the Wing

WILDLIFE IN THE SEA

As almost 90% of the Isle of Man's territory is underwater, there is a wealth of marine wildlife to be found in Manx seas. As well as fabulous underwater caves, eelgrass meadows and rocky reefs, there are many species of large, charismatic creatures which inhabit the Isle of Man's coastline and at times come in very close to shore, making them easy to spot from land.

Inquisitive grey seals, majestic basking sharks, graceful dolphins and other marine animals are drawn here not only to feed but by relatively clean, nutrient-rich water, warmed by the Gulf stream and sheltered from the harsh Atlantic Ocean.

The following is a guide to some of the more common species and where and when to go for the best chance of seeing them. Under the Wildlife Act, 1990, all are protected from intentional or reckless harm and disturbance. It is hoped that through this protection and good conservation measures, these amazing creatures will continue to thrive in Manx waters.

ATLANTIC GREY SEALS

Given that there are two seal species seen around Britain, you'd expect by virtue of its name that the common seal would be a more frequent sight than the Atlantic grey. Yet the opposite is true. In fact, around half of the world's population of grey seals live around Britain, and it's thought that about 6,000 inhabit the Irish Sea.

Seals used to be hunted in Britain for their fur and the oil in their blubber and, although grey seal population numbers are now recovering, they are still at risk from other threats, such as entanglement in fishing gear.

Grey seals are large animals – the largest land-going carnivore in Britain – with males weighing up to 300 kg. They are also remarkable swimmers, easily covering the distance between the Isle of Man and Ireland, Scotland, England or Wales. Although they regularly haul themselves on to rocks to rest, seals spend about 80% of their time in the water, so can most definitely be considered marine mammals.

Grey seals can stay underwater for up to something like 15 minutes, diving regularly to depths of around 80 metres. Their eyesight is good but their hearing is excellent, and their sensitive whiskers are vital for catching prey in the often murky waters. They tend to hunt near the seabed and feed on a wide variety of fish, crustaceans and even squid and octopus. Expressed another way, grey seals are far better suited for life at sea than on land, where they look cumbersome and ungainly. Their flippers, ideally suited for graceful underwater swimming, are not designed for walking on land – and especially their hind flippers, which point backwards! Hence a grey seal's time on land is restricted to hauling itself on to a suitable rock to dry, warm up and rest.

Grey seals do though give birth on land – a sheltered beach or a cave, typically in autumn and to a single, white fluffy pup. The distinctive white coat is a throwback to

Atlantic grey seals: bulky and limbless yet very adept at hauling themselves on to rocks to rest and warm up. Easily and frequently seen on Kitterland in the Sound (south).

Unlike other dolphins, Risso's feed mainly on squid, octopus and cuttlefish.

the ice age, when pups would have been well camouflaged on land covered in snow and ice. Born tiny and helpless, a pup quickly fattens up on its mother's milk, which is extremely rich in fat – more than 50%, compared with only about 4% in cow's milk. During this time, male seals patrol the pupping beaches, waiting for the females to wean their pups, become receptive again and mate. Only the biggest, strongest males will be able to fight the others off and win the chance to mate. A female feeds her pup for only about 3 weeks before weaning it and leaving it to fend for itself. It's a difficult start to life for a young seal and only the fittest survive. However, those that make it can live for at least 30 years.

GREY SEALS AROUND THE ISLE OF MAN

Grey seals inhabit Isle of Man coastal waters all through the year, but there are more around in summer months and several locations where you're almost guaranteed to see them.

The best place of all is the Sound, the stretch of water at the south-west tip, between the main island and the nearby Calf of Man. At low tide sometimes as many as a hundred seals bask on the rocks of the small islet within the Sound known as Kitterland. They are easy to spot, particular for visitors to the nearby but unobtrusive Sound Visitor Centre and cafe.

Other reliable places to see seals are around Peel Castle and breakwater in the west, Langness in the south, the Ayres in the north and Maughold Head in the north-east. And as well as seals resting on rocks, look out too for heads bobbing in the water.

WHALES, DOLPHINS AND PORPOISES

Collectively, these marine species are known as cetaceans, which comes from the ancient Greek for 'sea monsters'. Cetaceans are true marine mammals, spending their entire lives at sea, including resting, mating and giving birth in the water. As mammals, they have to come to the surface to breathe and this is usually the only glimpse into their lives that we are privileged to experience.

Cetaceans show even more adaptations to a life at sea than do seals, reflecting their exclusively marine lifestyle. They have streamlined bodies that lack hair – features designed by nature to reduce drag through the water. The tail has adapted into a horizontal fluke, giving powerful propulsion through the water, and the thick layer of body blubber keeps them warm.

Broadly speaking, cetaceans can be divided into two classes – those with teeth (odontocetes) and those without (mysticetes). All dolphins and porpoises are odontocetes, using their teeth to catch fish, whereas the typically larger whales are mysticetes. Instead of teeth, whales have baleen plates which hang down from their upper jaw inside the mouth. Made of keratin, these plates are much like human hair and fingernails, and act as combs to filter out the krill and small fish that whales feed on.

Odontocetes boast another and truly remarkable adaptation – the sense of echolocation. They produce sound waves which echo back from objects, such as prey, enabling dolphins and porpoises to build up a 'picture' of the surrounding area – a vital ability in dark, deep or murky waters in which eyesight is of little use. And as sound travels four times faster in water than it does in air, odontocetes have learned to capitalise on this great and very necessary ability.

Some species possess echolocation which is so precise that they can discriminate between not only objects of different shapes and sizes but also texture, and their distance away. And dolphins are considered incredibly intelligent, rivalling chimpanzees in brain power. They can solve complex problems, use tools and communicate using what is

considered to be virtually a language. Dolphins are also one of a very few groups of animals which have developed individual 'cultures' in individual populations. These skills are passed down through the generations, not through genes but through teaching. For example, mother dolphins in a region in Australia teach their offspring to use sponges to protect their beaks when hunting amongst the sharp corals.

Several species of cetaceans have been recorded in Manx waters and the wider Irish Sea, including bottlenose dolphin, common dolphin, killer whale, fin whale and humpback whale. However, by far the most likely species you can see around the island are harbour porpoise, Risso's dolphin and minke whale.

HARBOUR PORPOISE

The smallest and most common cetacean in British waters, harbour porpoise are about 2 metres long when fully grown. All porpoise species are distinct from their dolphin cousins by virtue of spade-shaped teeth as opposed to the conical-shaped teeth of dolphins. Porpoise are also distinctive for a rounded head, small 'beak' and small triangular-shaped dorsal fin. Their body is a uniform dark grey, with a paler underside – counter-shading which is common in marine species as it gives good camouflage from both above and below.

The diet of harbour porpoise consists mainly of small, schooling fish such as sand eels, sprat and herring. They tend to hunt near the seabed, making them vulnerable to being caught in the fishing nets of bottom trawlers. Although they sometimes come together in groups to feed on a large helping of food, harbour porpoise are considered quite unsociable animals. They tend to be seen individually or in small groups of no more than four or five. However, like most mammals, there is a strong bond between mother and calf and they may stay together for up to a year.

Another distinctive feature of harbour porpoise is that they are not so acrobatic as some dolphins and rarely leap out of the water.

HARBOUR PORPOISE AROUND THE ISLE OF MAN

Harbour porpoise are by far the most common cetacean seen around the Isle of Man. As it is thought that they do not travel huge distances, it is likely there is a year-round resident population and this, combined with the fact that they are the top predators in the area, makes the species an important indicator of the health of Manx waters.

Although common, harbour porpoise are quite difficult to spot because of their small size and brief surfacing. But on a calm day, three locations in particular – Marine Drive (Douglas), Niarbyl and the Sound – give you a good chance of seeing them. The most reliable place of all is off the Ledges, in Port St Mary, where they sometimes come within a hundred metres of the shore.

RISSO'S DOLPHINS

Risso's are unusual and little-studied dolphins, as they are usually found only in deep offshore waters. However, around the Isle of Man they come in very close to shore. They are large and robust, growing to a length of about 4 metres, and like harbour porpoise do not have a beak so the head looks blunt and bulbous.

But the most striking feature of a Risso's dolphin is its colouring. Although as a juvenile it is dark grey, it accumulates white scars as it ages and older specimens can be almost white all over. These scars are the joint result of fighting amongst themselves and strikes inflicted by prey trying to defend itself.

Another unusual feature is that unlike that of other dolphins, a Risso's diet is composed mainly of squid, octopus and cuttlefish (collectively called cephalopods), and the tentacles of these cephalopods are the cause of some of the Risso's scarring patterns. As cephalopods do not have any bones, a Risso's dolphin has no real need for many teeth and typically has only six pairs remaining, and only in the lower jaw. And as its prey is typically found in deep waters, a Risso's is capable of diving to about 300 metres and holding its breath for up to 30 minutes.

RISSO'S DOLPHINS AROUND THE ISLE OF MAN

Risso's dolphins are relatively easy to identify by virtue of their size, tall dorsal fin and unusual colouring. They are normally seen in Manx waters from spring – on the east coast – through to late summer. As the season progresses, they tend to move further south and by August you are more likely to spot them around the Calf of Man. Good locations for seeing them are Marine Drive (Douglas), Langness, Port St Mary ledges and the Sound.

MINKE WHALES

The smallest of the baleen whales, minkes grow up to about 8 metres long. Although typically grey, with a white underside, they are unique in having a white band on their front flippers and also distinctive for a head which is unusually triangular in shape.

Despite their large size, minke whales can swim relatively quickly, reaching speeds of up to 20 mph. They are also capable of migrating large distances, although currently it is not known how far they range in the Irish Sea. But minkes are found as far north as the polar seas, where they feed on the abundant krill and small fish, such as herring, which make up the majority of their diet.

Minke whales tend to be fairly solitary, although they sometimes come together in groups to feed on a large patch of prey. They can be acrobatic too, often scooping up whole shoals of fish by lunging out of the water – sometimes completely – with mouths wide open.

Being the smallest of the whales, minkes were not hunted as much as other species, although as the larger whales were depleted they were targeted more. They are still hunted today by countries such as Japan and Norway, although it is not thought that their population faces a high threat.

MINKE WHALES AROUND THE ISLE OF MAN

Minke whales are usually seen off the Manx coastline from June until about October. In summer you can spot them off the west coast, sometimes a few miles offshore, but good places to see them from land are Niarbyl and Bradda Head.

In autumn they move round to the east coast, probably following the herring to their spawning grounds, and are often seen around Laxey and Bulgham bays.

Much larger than a dolphin or porpoise, a minke whale is also distinctive for its dorsal fin, located about two thirds of the way down its back. So when a minke surfaces, first you will see an arched back, the dorsal fin's appearance delayed.

BASKING SHARKS

Basking sharks are a hugely popular and fascinating attraction to Isle of Man residents and visitors. The largest fish in British waters, and globally second only in size to tropical whale sharks, basking sharks can grow to 12 metres long – about the same length as a double-decker bus. More typically though, the largest are around 8-10 metres and weigh in at roughly 7 tonnes – as much as two fully-grown elephants. Basking sharks which frequent Isle of Man waters are mostly 4-7 metres long, exceptions being occasionally-seen newborns of 1.5 metres at one end of the scale and imposing 10-metre specimens at the other.

In fact, just about every dimension of a basking shark is impressive. Its dorsal fin, in the middle of its back, can be two metres high and its mouth over a metre wide. It has about 1500 tiny teeth, and almost completely encircling the huge head are 5 gill slits. The only small features of a basking shark are its eyes and brain.

Basking sharks are one of the group of fishes called elasmobranches, to which other sharks, skates and rays also belong. Elasmobranch skeletons are not made of bone but cartilage, and there is no swim bladder, buoyancy provided instead by a large oil-filled liver. Sadly, in the past, this oil has commanded a high commercial value – one of the reasons why basking sharks were so actively hunted.

Nor do elasmobranches have scales. Their skin is composed of millions of denticles – small teeth-like plates, all running in the same direction and overlapping each other so that the skin is smooth one way but very rough the other, rather like sandpaper, and it has rippled blue-grey patterns which resemble those on mackerel skin.

Yet despite their huge size and the enormous interest which basking sharks inspire, very little is known about many aspects of their biology. Questions such as how long they live and where they breed and give birth are yet to be answered, and Manx Wildlife Trust's Basking Shark Watch project aims to play an important role in filling the gaps in our current knowledge and understanding of these gentle and fascinating marine giants. What *is* well known is that they are found throughout the world in temperate, mainly coastal waters.

Basking sharks come to Manx waters primarily to eat. They feed exclusively on zoo-plankton – a rich mixture of microscopic shrimp, fish eggs and larvae, their favourite food being a family of small shrimps called calanus copepods. The sharks' feeding method, known as obligate ram feeding, is unique, swimming slowly, mouth

Up to 12 metres long and as heavy as two fully-grown elephants, basking sharks can leap completely out of the water – a spectacle sometimes seen close to the Isle of Man coastline.

wide open. Water flows in and exits via gill slits which are lined with comb-like gill rakers to filter the plankton. When there's sufficient plankton to warrant swallowing it, the mouth closes. In just an hour, a basking shark can filter the amount of water it takes to fill an Olympic-sized swimming pool, yielding about 30 kg of plankton in the process.

It is possible that basking sharks come to the Isle of Man to socialise too – maybe even to mate and give birth. They exhibit various types of behaviour, called social swimming, which are thought to be associated with courtship. For example, pairs or groups of sharks circle or follow each other very closely, nose to tail, and sometimes leap completely out of the water, just off the coast – a real wow factor spectacle should you be lucky enough to witness it at first hand.

Basking sharks give birth to live young, which hatch from eggs inside the female's uterus. The developing young sharks are nourished by the other unhatched eggs and are born able to swim, and even to feed on their own. It is thought that at birth baby sharks are about 1.5 -2 metres long, their snub piggy-like nose making them easy to identify. Basking sharks of this sort of size have been sighted and reported on the Isle of Man, supporting the idea that they may indeed give birth here.

A HIGHLY ENDANGERED SPECIES

Although on the Isle of Man you can see these amazing animals so close inshore, scientists estimate that the world population of breeding females could be as low as 8,000.

Basking sharks are found in temperate waters all around the globe – Europe, the Mediterranean, North and South America, New Zealand and Taiwan. In most of the world it is illegal to fish for them or to sell any basking shark product, but illicit trade in shark fins continues and fishing is still allowed in some countries..

In the past, basking sharks were hunted nearly to extinction for their oil. Now the main dangers they face are accidental entanglement in fishing nets or rope and being hunted and killed for their enormous fins, used in making shark fin soup. These activities are unsustainable, as experts believe that basking sharks breed very slowly, pregnancies lasting maybe 3 years and producing 5 or 6 offspring.

BASKING SHARKS AROUND THE ISLE OF MAN

Basking sharks are attracted to Manx waters in summer months, typically from mid-May until the end of August. But every year the pattern is slightly different, good numbers of sightings sometimes starting at the beginning of May or going right through until the end of September. Generally speaking, the most reliable months for shark watching are June and July.

True to their name, they appear to be basking in the sun as they feed or socialise on the surface. The vast majority of sightings occur in a 40-km stretch of the western coast between Peel and the Calf of Man, where it is thought that the greatest accumulations of plankton occur. Good places from which to see the sharks include Peel Castle, Niarbyl, Port Erin bay and the Sound.

Your best chance of seeing basking sharks is on calm and sunny days. More sharks are at the surface, and it's also much easier to spot their fins in the water than it is when conditions are choppy. The first sign of a basking shark is usually its big triangular dorsal fin, appearing above the water, the sun reflecting off its wet skin. Often you can see the top of the tail fin, and even the tip of the nose as the shark breaks surface. And if you're in an elevated location, such as a cliff top, and the water's clear, you may even see the shape of the whole body underwater – a truly magnificent and unforgettable sight.

Most basking shark sightings reported to Manx Basking Shark Watch are within just a kilometre of the shore. Sometimes they come closer still, swimming right into bays and alongside piers and outcrops. Binoculars are an advantage but you can often see them with the naked eye.

They are attracted when their food, tiny zooplankton, concentrates at the surface, which occurs when the sea stratifies into layers of different temperatures and produces tidal fronts – long shiny lines in the water. The highest concentrations of the oil-rich plankton are found in these fronts, which also attract diving gannets – a good indication that basking sharks may be present.

You can get even closer to basking sharks by booking a seat aboard a wildlife watching boat operating from Port St Mary, Port Erin or Peel, where most of these boats are based. Details are available from the harbourside Welcome Centre in Douglas or online.

The Isle of Man has taken significant steps to ensure that basking sharks enjoy the protection of the law. Targeted fishing, and even accidental disturbance, are offences, and although you can scuba dive or snorkel with them it is vital for the safety of the sharks and yourself that you observe and adhere to the Shark Trust's Code of Conduct, which is on the Trust's website. Dive boats for these activities operate under strict and very carefully controlled conditions. For details contact the Welcome Centre in Douglas.

MANX BASKING SHARK WATCH

Scientists on the Isle of Man are ideally placed to study basking sharks. Manx Basking Shark Watch has been working with local government and scientists worldwide to uncover more facts about these animals.

MBSW is a charitable project of Manx

Basking sharks are most easily seen on calm sunny days. The best locations from which to look out for them include Peel Castle, Niarbyl, Port Erin bay and the Sound.

Wildlife Trust, operated by volunteers and heavily dependent on funding from private and government sponsorship and grants. You can help with this work too, either as a volunteer or by reporting your basking shark sightings, photographs and stories to Manx Basking Shark Watch at www.manx baskingsharkwatch. com.

All reported sightings are of great value to the few Isle of Man-based scientists currently engaged in the basking shark study. Between 2005-2010 nearly 800 people contributed information to MBSW. Manx Wildlife Trust also organises effort-based watchers, an initiative whereby many hours are spent at key hot spots recording sightings of basking sharks, whales, dolphins, porpoises, seals and birds.

This activity, together with reported sightings to MBSW, has already led to many fascinating discoveries. Maps have been produced showing where most sharks are seen, and sightings and photographs include courtship behaviour and newborn basking sharks, which have contributed to many

aspects of MBSW's scientific work. All public sightings data is shared with other scientists and with the UK's Marine Conservation Society Basking Shark Sighting Scheme.

BASKING SHARK PASSPORTS

An obvious difficulty of a public sighting scheme of this nature is that the same shark is reported repeatedly and there is no way of knowing if the same sharks are coming back year after year. With genetic work suggesting a very small world population, MBSW decided to identify individual sharks so that they could be re-identified again and again, allowing a much better estimate of shark numbers in Manx and British waters and determining whether the same animals are staying for long and whether they do indeed visit year after year.

To address these issues, each basking shark is now given a 'passport'. This comprises high-definition photographs of the right and left side of the big dorsal fin, the shark's sex (determined with a pole camera), estimated size of the shark, and its DNA, for which a swab is taken from the dorsal fin.

This work began in earnest in 2009 and by the end of 2010 the fin observations had identified 86 individual sharks, some of which have been seen again and again – one as many as 5 times. Another was spotted in Manx waters for 3 consecutive years. A further 10 years of this invaluable work should yield an effective catalogue and far greater understanding of these esoteric animals.

The genetic work is still in its infancy but has revealed that the fin ID method works well and that the population is highly inbred – an unsurprising fact, given the intensive hunting in the past for basking sharks and the resultant drastic drop in their global population. This information also highlights and urges the need for increased conservation and protection measures worldwide.

TAGGING STUDIES

Until recently, seasonal movements of basking sharks were something of a mystery – seen in inshore waters for a few months every summer and occasionally caught in deep-water trawls in winter, but otherwise where they went or why was unknown.

Scientists are now slowly unravelling these mysteries, and one of the techniques employed is tagging (the most commonly used are MK10 PAT archival tags, but other types are being developed). Before tagging it was thought that during winter basking sharks lay on the seabed, hibernating, but scientists tagging basking sharks off Cornwall discovered that they go to deeper waters off the continental shelf and continue feeding all winter.

Further work by American scientists revealed that basking sharks tagged close to Newfoundland travelled to the Caribbean and even as far south as Brazil, crossing the equator. So it appears that at least some of the basking sharks attracted to Manx waters

could be global travellers, possibly frequenting regions where they are not protected from hunting and disturbance, as they are in the North Atlantic.

Between 2007 and 2009, Manx Basking Shark Watch tagged 16 basking sharks. This included an 8 metre-long female (subsequently given the name Tracy) which surprised everyone by crossing the Atlantic – a 10,000-kilometre marathon from Peel to Newfoundland, Canada – and diving to over 1200 metres, all in just 82 days. (Source: '*Transatlantic migration and deep mid-ocean diving by basking shark*' by Mauvis Gore, et al. Published in *Biological Letters* code 10.1098/rsbl.2008. 0147.)

MBSW's tagging operation to discover more about basking shark movements is continuing.

COURTSHIP STUDIES

Close social swimming by basking sharks – less than half a shark body length apart – is often seen, sometimes in line and other times side by side in an echelon formation. Tails are thrashed, stand-offs are observed and, most spectacular of all, some large sharks leap clear of the water, acting more like salmon than the leviathans they are.

Many scientists and Isle of Man boat owners are convinced that these types of behaviour are shows of courtship. Very close parallel swimming with tail thrashing has been seen and could well be mating – an event never photographed.

Manx Basking Shark Watch is taking HD video and still photography in an attempt to further understand basking shark behaviour. If it transpires that they are indeed mating in Manx waters, the close protection afforded by the Manx government is not only fully justified but more important than ever.

HABITAT AND SPECIES CONSERVATION AND PROTECTION

THE WORK OF MANX WILDLIFE TRUST

Based in Peel, Manx Wildlife Trust is an independent charity caring for the island's land, sea and freshwater environments and sharply focused on habitat and species conservation and protection.

Key to this work is the acquisition and management of nature trails and reserves. Currently (2012), there are 22 of these sites across the Isle of Man, of which 11 are open to the public and give you free access. All 22 are described in the following pages.

Manx Wildlife Trust works in partnership with many other similar wildlife charities based throughout the British Isles. In addition to habitat and species protection, the Trust promotes local environmental awareness, promotes and conducts scientific research and offers ecological advice and expertise.

To contact Manx Wildlife Trust, call 01624 844432, or email enquiries@ manxwt.org.uk, or call into the Wildlife Shop at 7-8 Market Place, Peel.

THE COUNTRY CODE

When visiting the highly sensitive environments of Manx Wildlife Trust nature reserves and trails, it is particularly important to please observe the Country Code at all times.

■ Enjoy the countryside and respect its life and work.

■ Guard against all risk of fire.

■ Fasten all gates.

■ Keep dogs on a lead, and no fouling.

■ Keep to public paths across farmland.

■ Use gates and styles to cross fences, hedges and walls.

■ Leave livestock, crops and machinery alone.

■ Take your litter home.

■ Help to keep all water clean.

■ Protect wildlife, plants and trees.

■ Take special care on country roads.

■ Make no unnecessary noise.

NATURE RESERVES AND TRAILS YOU CAN VISIT

All of the following Manx Wildlife Trust sites are open to the public and give you free access. For easy reference they are listed in alphabetical order by name rather than by location.

AYRES VISITOR CENTRE & NATURE TRAIL

Map reference: NX 435038.

The Ayres Visitor Centre lies within an important stretch of low-lying sand dune coastline which runs for 8 km from Cronk-y-Bing to the Point of Ayre. The area is of major ecological significance, parts having been designated an Area of Special Scientific Interest and the only National Nature Reserve on the Isle of Man. The land is jointly owned by the government's Department of Environment, Food and Agriculture, and Manx National Heritage.

Manx Wildlife Trust established the Visitor Centre and Nature Trail here to increase public understanding of this vulnerable area, and to provide information about its birds, habitats and rare plant communities. The Nature Trail leads you from the shingle beach through the marram dunes and on to the expanse of heath, which has extensive lichen flora. Every stage of the trail is full of variety and interest.

Sea-watching from the shore can be very

The Ayres – vulnerable sand dune coastline within which are an Area of Special Scientific Interest, the Ayres Visitor Centre and the island's only National Nature Reserve.

rewarding. In summer you can watch diving gannets and terns offshore, with the exciting prospect of seeing basking sharks, seals and other marine mammals, and at any time of year there's an impressive variety of seabirds and waders on view.

Move inland and you'll see that marram and other plants colonise the upper shore. The fixed dunes have their own distinct communities of plants and insects, notably the spectacular displays of burnet rose and pyramidal orchids. Further inland again is the heath and its rare lichens, nesting stonechats, oystercatchers and lapwings, and busy insect populations.

The Ayres is a highly sensitive and wild environment, and nowhere on the Isle of Man is the Country Code more relevant and important. Fires, vehicles and dogs can all cause serious damage to this beautiful and rare landscape.

The Ayres Visitor Centre has an adjacent car park and is signposted on the Ballaghennie Road, west of Bride. It opens from Tuesday to Sunday inclusive, 2.00 pm–5.00 pm, from the end of May to the end of September.

BALLALOUGH REEDBEDS
Map reference: SC 258682.
Size: 1.5 hectares (3.66 acres).
Habitats: reedbed and meadow.
Notable species: common reed (*Phragmites australis*), false fox-sedge (*Carex otrubae*) and common spotted orchid.

This reserve comprises two fields divided by a traditional Manx sod hedge which is lined with hawthorn. The fields lie lower than the surrounding land and this, together with a ditch, is sufficient to maintain quite a high water table and create the right conditions for the growth of common reed, which occurs as a strip around the northern edge of the two fields.

This type of habitat, very susceptible to drainage, is extremely rare on the Isle of Man and covers just 0.03% of the land area.

Reedbeds are an important and valuable wildlife habitat, supporting insects, other invertebrates and frogs, as well as a variety of specialist birds which include willow warbler, sedge warbler and reed bunting.

Grassland occupies the remainder of the fields, the more westerly being fairly dry but the other quite wet. It is here, unusually, that you can see large quantities of false fox sedge, which is normally found near the coast. The meadow and wetland are rich in wild flowers, species including ragged robin, greater bird's-foot trefoil, vetches, red clover, meadow vetchling, marsh woundwort, marsh cinquefoil, meadowsweet and wild angelica.

In 1998 Manx Wildlife Trust received a grant from the Rees Jeffreys Road Fund which financed not only the fencing of the reserve but also the creation of a small parking area and the planting of a hedge of native shrubs. The reserve is managed to maintain and enhance this valuable and rare habitat, the grassland cut annually in the drier of the two fields.

The reserve has a small car park and is readily accessible from the Castletown by-pass (A5), which forms the reserve's southern boundary.

BREAGLE GLEN, PORT ERIN
Map reference: SC 196688.
Size: 0.3 hectares (0.8 acres).
Habitats: urban, comprising small woodland, developing woodland and an area of shrub which bears berries and nectar.
Notable species: a variety of migrant birds including yellow-browed warbler.

The reserve consists of a small valley with a stream and an elevated area, part of which is devoted to nectar and berry species, the remainder planted in 2005 with native trees and shrub. A narrow strip of grassland alongside the pavement is mown regularly.

The valley woodland is a small but important link in a chain of woodland cover for birds. Good numbers of familiar species such as blackbird, goldcrest, robin and willow warbler are seen regularly. The glen also acts as a resting and stopping-off point for migrants, notable species of which include barred warbler, firecrest, lesser whitethroat and pied and red-breasted flycatchers.

Management of the reserve is a year-round task requiring regular clearance around the trees and shrubs and applying copious quantities of compost which is made on another reserve. The ongoing planting of berry-bearing and nectar-bearing shrubs aims to attract birds, butterflies and other insects.

The reserve is readily accessible from St George's Crescent, which forms the entire north and west boundaries.

CLOSE SARTFIELD, BALLAUGH

Map reference: SC 361956.
Size: 12.6 hectares (31 acres).
Habitats: damp hay meadows, marshy grassland, curragh (willow scrub) and developing birch woodland. The curragh is interspersed with open areas of bog myrtle on a deep substrate of peat.
Notable flora species: Six species of orchids (May to July), royal fern, bog myrtle and yellow bartsia.
Notable bird species: corncrake and hen harrier.

Excellent for birdwatching, Close Sartfield lies on the north-west edge of the Ballaugh Curragh, the Isle of Man's largest wetland. From the car park to the bird hide, the reserve is open to the public all year round. The path/nature trail through the remainder of the site is open from the beginning of June to the end of August. Level paths and boardwalks provide wheelchair access to the bird hide, but no dogs are allowed.

A variety of small birds depends on the many invertebrates that thrive amongst the rich flora and in the soft wet ground. These birds are in turn targeted by birds of prey

and by stoats and other predators.

Breeding species within the reserve include lesser redpoll, grasshopper warbler, reed bunting, sedge warbler, whitethroat, curlew and – it is thought – water rail. Hen harriers are seen frequently throughout the year and the hide is well sited to observe their evening return to a midwinter roost. From the hide you could also be lucky enough to see a peregrine or a merlin. In 1999, 2000 and 2006, corncrakes were sighted on the reserve.

The flora of the hay meadows is outstanding, and from late May to July tens of thousands of orchids are in bloom, species including heath spotted, early marsh, common spotted, northern marsh and common twayblade. Amongst the other grassland species present are yellow bartsia, yellow rattle, lousewort, purple loosestrife and cuckooflower. In the areas of peat, bog myrtle and purple moor grass are dominant, and other plants of the wetter areas include bog-bean, marsh cinquefoil, devil's bit scabious and cotton-grass. In autumn, the colour of the magnificent bushy royal fern – the largest of the British ferns – is a beautiful orange.

Grey willow is dominant in the scrub, and downy birch is also becoming well established. Other trees present in the reserve include holly, sycamore, ash and wych elm. In 1991, a copse of alders was planted in the long meadow.

You can get to Close Sartfield from the TT course (A3) by turning on to the B9 between Ballaugh village and Sulby Glen. Take the third turn on the right and follow the road for nearly a mile. The reserve entrance and car park are along a nearby track which is less than 100 yards on the right.

COOILDARRY, KIRK MICHAEL

Map reference: 314901.
Size: 7.29 hectares (17.5 acres).
Habitats: woodland and river.
Notable species: cow parsley (uncommon

The Ballaugh Curragh Nature Trail reveals the story of the woodland's development and the history of the area's land use.

on the Isle of Man), greater horsetail and wood warbler.

Cooildarry derives its name from darragh (oak tree) and cooil (nook). It is a deep wooded valley forming the upper part of Glen Wyllin, through which the Ballalonna river runs in a series of waterfalls over an ancient bed of Manx slates. More than 50 species of birds have been recorded here, and 35 (including raven and sparrowhawk) breed in the area.

The present woodland owes its character to planting in the Victorian era, though it has some semi-natural characteristics. Today the canopy is varied, the dominant species being elm, ash, alder, sycamore and beech. Other trees present include oak, chestnut, lime, hazel, silver birch, hawthorn,

blackthorn and holly.

Exotic species are here too, such as rhododendron, Portugal and cherry laurel, and Corsican pine. Mosses, liverworts, horsetails and ferns all grow in profusion in the moist shady conditions.

Over 50 species of fungi have been recorded. In spring, the woodland floor is carpeted with primrose, wood anemone, wood sorrel, lesser celandine and bluebell. Opposite-leaved golden saxifrage spreads freely over the moister areas. Boggy patches in the valley floor, more open to sunlight, support yellow flag, hemlock water dropwort and branched bur-reed.

In management terms, for many years the main task for Manx Wildlife Trust at this site was to reinstate some of the paths, including sections of boardwalk and a number of

---

bridges, and most of the current work concentrates on maintaining these facilities in a safe condition, although attempts have been made to also reinstate two ornamental ponds.

At present, work on trees is confined to wind damage and those which overhang a footpath or are felt to pose a danger. All wood is left on site to rot. Where it is safe to do so, standing or fallen dead wood is left to decay in situ for fungi and beetles. The future aim is to undertake more active woodland management, in particular controlling rhododendron and sycamore.

There are two entrances to Cooildarry. One is opposite the road to Glen Wyllin campsite on the Peel to Kirk Michael Road. Parking is available at the top of the road to the campsite. The other entrance is on the TT course, one mile south-east of Kirk Michael. You can park in a small lay-by. Please note that dogs must be kept on a lead, and no fouling.

CRONK Y BING, ANDREAS

Map reference: NX 381017.
Size: 12.6 hectares (31 acres).
Habitats: sand dunes and shingle foreshore, waterside at the mouth of the Lhen Trench.
Notable species: Isle of Man cabbage and pyramidal orchid, oysterplant, dune fescue and little tern.

This reserve is situated near the southern tip of the Ayres – an area of unique heathland and sand dune. Cronk y Bing has one of the island's widest strips of yellow dune. In the past, sand has been extracted from the back dunes, forming a flatter area behind the leading dunes and upon which has developed coastal grassland, grazed by rabbits.

Marram grass (bent) dominates, the variety of other plant species including pyramidal orchid, sea bindweed, restharrow, common stork's-bill, bugloss, harebell, sheep's-bit, wild carrot, common cornsalad, burnet rose and wild mignonette. On the

shore you will find sea holly and saltwort.

The Lhen Trench is a largely canalised river, draining part of the Ballaugh Curragh, and has a variety of additional species including water mint, hemlock water dropwort, marsh woundwort, cudweed, angelica, marsh bedstraw and figwort. The adjacent shoreline is a favoured breeding ground for little terns and other birds such as oystercatchers, ringed plovers and meadow pipits. Often seen in autumn are divers, grebes, sea ducks, skuas, waders and a variety of gulls. Off the coast you could see seals, basking sharks and diving gannets.

Management of the reserve monitors erosion and accretion. Cushag (common ragwort) is removed from the site and rubbish collected regularly from the dunes.

Cronk y Bing is accessible from the A10 by taking the track to the beach immediately south of the Lhen Bridge (map reference NX 379013). The Isle of Man coastal footpath (Raad Ny Foillan – Road of the Gull) runs along the shore section of the reserve. Parking space is at the seaward end of the track. Please note that dogs must be kept on a lead, and no fouling.

CURRAGH KIONDROGHAD, ONCHAN

Map reference: SC400782.
Size: 0.4 hectares (1 acre).
Habitats: wetland of curragh (willow scrub), broadleaved trees, dub (pond), neutral grassland, embankments of tall grassland. Minor habitats include ditches, tall swamp vegetation and tall ruderal vegetation.

This wetland reserve is a green oasis hemmed in by houses and is only two minutes' walk from the shopping centre in Onchan. Nearly one hundred species of flowering plants flourish here, from wetland to woodland varieties. Mainly grey, and some white, willow dominates the wetlands.

Other wetland plants include marsh marigold, yellow flag, reed canary grass, hemlock water-dropwort, woody nightshade and cuckooflower. The woody stems of the grey willow support a variety of mosses and lichens. Liverworts are present on ditch banks. Trees common at the perimeter of the reserve, where it is drier, include silver birch, ash, holly and rowan, and as for hedgerow plant species you can see red campion, herb-robert, ivy, ferns and others.

A mixed hedgerow of hawthorn, blackthorn, dog rose, hazel, field maple and wild privet has been planted. The reserve has rich invertebrate life, which supports many bird species and bats. Grey wagtail, goldcrest, woodcock, chiffchaff and hen harrier, together with more common garden bird species, have all been recorded on site. In spring, frogs return to breed.

Management of the reserve is focused on controlling the vigorous regeneration of sycamore, as this is not a native species. The grassland is cut regularly in summer months and the dub is kept clear by regular dredging.

You can get to this wetlands reserve from the A2. Near Onchan, turn into Church Road and as it dips park on your left. The entrance to the reserve is across a piece of land on your left, and a boardwalk enables wheelchair access. Please note: dogs must be kept on a lead, and no fouling.

DALBY MOUNTAIN MOORLAND
Map reference: SC 233769.
Size: 28 hectares (69 acres).
Habitats: wet and dry dwarf shrub heath, marshy grassland and scrub.
Notable species: breeding red grouse, hen harrier, bog asphodel and heath spotted orchid.

Manx Wildlife Trust acquired this threatened site to prevent destruction of the moorland habitats, as it was feared that the area was liable to be planted with conifers to link adjoining plantations. The reserve – traditional heath moorland comprising 5% of the Isle of Man's wet heath – is in fact sandwiched between two conifer plantations

and bisected by the A27 road and a public footpath.

Heather, purple moor grass and rushes with locally-abundant bog asphodel dominate the wet heath. Other species include devil's bit scabious, cross-leaved heath and heath spotted orchids. The dry heath is dominated by bell heather, ling/heather and western gorse. In addition to grouse and hen harrier, you could well see snipe and curlew. Adder's tongue fern was found on the roadside verge in 1996.

Dalby Mountain is managed within the southern uplands heath. Blocks of heather are controlled in rotation to create a mosaic of heather stands of different ages. Burning is governed by a code of practice and there are further restrictions on the reserve due to the proximity of the plantations. The wet heath is not burned.

The A27 (Dalby to Round Table) passes through the reserve. There is off-road parking space at the point on the west side of the road where a track to Eary Cushlin commences. Please note: dogs must be kept on a lead, and no fouling. Shooting on the reserve is prohibited.

EARYSTANE, COLBY
Map reference: SC 235715.
Size: 0.65 hectares (1.6 acres).
Habitats: moaney (willow scrub), broadleaved trees and shrubs, gorse scrub, ruderal vegetation and neutral grassland.

Originally part of Ballachrink (which in Manx Gaelic means hill farm), the site was sold to Arbory Parish Commissioners and half of it used as a tip until the 1970s.

Willows (predominantly grey willow) colonised the wetter low-lying part of the site and many branches are festooned with mosses and lichens. A great diversity of plants such as ground ivy, bluebells, marsh marigold, marsh woundwort, marsh thistle, rushes and heath spotted orchid are also found here.

Wetland areas here in the south are

named moaney (Manx Gaelic for peaty) but in the north are called curragh. The tip surface is colonised by grassland and ruderal vegetation such as nettles and rosebay willowherb with encroaching scrub, particularly bramble and gorse.

In the meadow areas are grasses and wild flowers such as knapweed, bird's-foot trefoil and clovers. Blue and great tit, robin, blackbird, wren and pheasant are often present. Hen harrier, raven and chough also frequent the area. When they arrive in spring, willow warbler and chiffchaff can be heard more easily than they can be seen. In autumn and winter, redwing and fieldfare fly overhead and feed in adjacent fields.

The grassland area is managed as a small hay meadow, cut in spring and late summer with the vegetation raked off. The planted trees and shrubs require maintenance until they can survive unassisted. The curragh is left to develop naturally although non-native species, particularly Japanese knotweed, are controlled. A path suitable for wheelchairs leads to a bird hide and a boardwalk through the curragh.

To get to Earystane, follow the A7 from Ballabeg or Ballagawne, and at Colby take the A27, leading north uphill towards Ronague and the Round Table. Pass Colby Glen on your left and at the sharp right-hand bend is a road sign pointing to Earystane on the left. The wooden gate to the reserve is on the right of this minor road.

You can park on the wide section of the A27 (but definitely not where it is narrow) on the Earystane road, or in the field gateways. Please note: dogs must be kept on a lead, and no fouling.

GLEN DHOO, BALLAUGH

Map reference: SC 258682.
Size: 9.4 hectares (23.5 acres).
Habitats: regenerating woodland, wet and dry grassland, flushes and a stream.
Notable species: lemon-scented fern, heath

spotted orchid and aspen.

This reserve lies in the remote valley of Glen Dhoo, near the confluence of tributary streams, and is surrounded by the steep slopes of Slieau Curn, Slieau Dhoo and the area of Ballaugh Plantation. A public right of way passes through the reserve, terminating at the ruined house (or tholtan) a little higher up the valley.

Glen Dhoo means black or dark glen – appropriate when Slieau Curn casts its shadow late in the day. High on the hill slopes are hut circles, from the time when animals were taken to high pasture for the summer. The tholtan within the reserve is a reminder of a small farming community, which occupied this remote glen up until the late 19th century.

Beyond the top boundary of the reserve are the remains of a water mill and dam. The river at the tholtan is bridged by a long flagstone, typical of the old river crossings in the parish of Ballaugh. Lemon-scented fern is found along the river. Hen harrier, raven, stonechat and linnet breed in the area. Peregrines frequent the valley and herons have also been recorded along the river.

The boundary of the reserve has been fenced to allow grazing to take place and the site divided into a number of compartments, within which each is managed according to its particular needs.

A large proportion of the upper slopes have been taken over by gorse and bracken, and as the slopes are too steep for machine access they are currently left largely unmanaged. On some of the lower slopes, gorse and bracken are controlled by various means including cutting, chemical sprays and sheep grazing, the aim being to return these meadows to upland grassland. The aspen growing on the slopes of the small tributary stream have been fenced off to protect them from the grazing.

To get to Glen Dhoo, take the road to Ballaugh Glen – between the Raven pub and Ballaugh bridge – and you can drive as

Sand dunes along the north-west coast are a fragile and endangered environment, at the mercy of wind and sea.

far as the forestry car park. Walk the final mile along a green lane (Bayr Glass) which starts just below the car park and runs roughly parallel with the river. Please note: dogs must be kept on a lead, and no fouling.

SCARLETT NATURE TRAIL
Map reference: SC 258664.

Outstanding coastal scenery with spectacular limestone and volcanic rock formations make Scarlett unique – an absolute must-see attraction for visitors to the Isle of Man. Standing between the quarry (the source of the limestone which built Castletown) and the triple lime kilns on the shore is the old Mine Manager's office. This is now used primarily as an education resource for school groups, and it contains maps, diagrams and displays introducing the complex geology and fossil remains of the Scarlett peninsula and its rich

coastal flora and bird life.

You can see these features – and specifically the limestone pavements and volcanic rocks such as the Stack – along the Nature Trail which leads beyond the building. It's an exhilarating walk at any time of year, and especially when spring flowers (such as spring squill, thrift, bird's-foot trefoil and stonecrop) carpet the rocky outcrops and the turf. In summer you can see wheatears, stonechats and meadow pipits darting amongst the rocks, and the quarry lake attracts hawking swallows and martins. The bay too is alive with the sights and sounds of seabirds.

To get to Scarlett, turn down the coast road west of Castletown and the car park is by the disused quarry.

Habitat and Species Conservation and Protection

OTHER NATURE RESERVES

Although these reserves are not open to the public, the following A-Z guide provides insight into the scope of the ongoing work conducted by Manx Wildlife Trust in species and habitat conservation and protection.

Ballamooar Meadow (Jurby) is just an acre (0.4 hectares) in size. The habitats here are marshy grassland and curragh (willow scrub). Notable species are common spotted orchid, gipsywort and water plantain. More than 100 plant species have been recorded here. Meadowsweet is dominant and red fescue is the main grass. A variety of interesting beetles are present.

The reserve forms part of a larger area of curragh associated with the major waterway of the Lhen Trench to the south, and this seasonally-wet meadow includes an area of curragh on its eastern edge. Before it was acquired by Manx Wildlife Trust, the field had been neglected for years and was becoming rank. Now it is cut in late summer, when plants have flowered, set seed and the vegetation is raked off, and the spread of willow is controlled.

Barnell Reservoir (Patrick) is a wild bird sanctuary of 2.2 hectares/5.44 acres. The habitats are open water, broadleaved and coniferous woodland, developing reedbed and species-rich grassland. Notable species are smooth-stalked sedge and bats, and the reserve supports a whole web of life, from aquatic invertebrates to birds and bats. Of the 52 species of birds recorded here, at least 20 species breed in the reserve. Pipistrelle, whiskered and Daubenton's bats have been seen feeding on insects over the water.

The woodland is generally left unmanaged for nature to take its course and natural regeneration to proceed. Dead wood is left on site to benefit invertebrates. The vegetation on the reservoir dam embankment is cut annually around late summer/early autumn to encourage a variety of grassland and wetland plants, and to prevent scrub from taking over. In recent years Manx Wildlife Trust has undertaken extensive remedial works on the dam wall, including repairs to the overflow and the construction of an additional overflow channel.

Parts of the reservoir banks are covered in gorse and bracken but there are also areas of mixed woodland, dominated at the southern end by ash and elm, and at the northern end by Scots and hybrid pines and European larch. Luxuriant ferns thrive in the damp conditions and primroses are a feature in spring.

The reservoir was constructed in the 1880s and until the late 1940s supplied the water for Peel. An upland stream feeds the reservoir and the maximum water depth is 20 feet. A fascinating feature is the stone-built aqueduct, leat and culvert, built to divert the stream so that the water level in the reservoir could be lowered. Also within the reserve is a mine trail adit.

Close e Quayle (Lezayre) covers just under 10 hectares (4.4 acres) and the habitats are hay meadow, marshy grassland, curragh (willow scrub), bracken and developing aspen woodland. Notable species include orchids (marsh violet, common spotted, heath spotted and greater butterfly) and royal fern and aspen, both of which are rare on the Isle of Man. The reserve also has at least 2 notable beetles (*Calodera riparia* and *Bibloplectus spinosus*) and in 1995 the 200th species of Manx spider was recorded here.

The reserve's 5 fields are within a designated site of special ecological importance for nature conservation. Over 100 plant species have been identified, including lesser stitchwort, marsh cinquefoil, purple loosestrife, marsh pennywort, devil's bit scabious and gipsywort. Amongst the birds recorded to date are hen harrier, snipe, curlew, sparrowhawk, barn owl and moorhen.

Prior to purchase by Manx Wildlife Trust,

the fields had been neglected for some years and tussocks of purple moor grass and rushes had become dominant. Three of the fields are now managed as hay meadows, cut in late summer when the plants have flowered and set seed and the vegetation has been raked off by volunteers. Another field is left uncut for the benefit of invertebrates and the fifth is maintained to create a mosaic of managed and unmanaged grassland, and curragh – achieved by cutting the managed area and controlling bracken. The reserve's boundary is fenced to allow grazing by sheep over the whole site or within particular fields.

At **Close Umpson** (Ballaugh) the reserve embraces 0.72 hectares (1.78 acres) and the habitats comprise semi-improved neutral grassland, marshy grassland/bog communities, bracken and curragh (willow scrub). Notable species are adder's tongue fern, moonwort, royal fern and orchids (common spotted, heath spotted and twayblade). Near the entrance the vegetation is hay meadow type, but towards the south the field passes into peat bog. The varied flora also includes pignut, knapweed, tormentil, bog myrtle, bog asphodel and bog-bean.

Before acquisition by Manx Wildlife Trust to rescue it from the possibility of being drained, rotavated and reseeded, this meadow had been left unmanaged for some time and was known by local naturalists as the Adder's Tongue Field – the only known spot in the Ballaugh Curragh where this fern was found. The vegetation had become rank and invading scrub threatened the future of the ferns, orchids and other species.

In the drier northern part of the reserve the scrub was cleared, and the grassland is now cut annually (October) and the vegetation raked off by volunteers. Invading willow scrub has been selectively cleared from the wetter areas of the field and attempts are being made to control bracken.

The future aim is to clear more willow and birch to maintain the open habitats.

Curragh Feeagh (German) covers 2.42 hectares (6 acres). The habitats are curragh (willow scrub), damp hay meadow, heath, rank grassland and bracken, notable species being adder's tongue fern, ragged robin and common spotted and heath spotted orchid.

Curragh Feeagh is Gaelic for raven's marsh, and this small reserve is at the watershed of the tributaries of the River Neb and Glen Mooar. Occasionally, hen harrier and merlin are seen passing through the reserve and breeding species probably include willow warbler, whitethroat and reed bunting.

The western half of the reserve lies in the floor of the shallow valley and is waterlogged for much of the year. A small stream carries a steady trickle of water out of the reserve southwards towards Glen Helen. Dominating this boggy area are willow and tussocks of purple moor grass. Osier is also present in small quantities, as are bracken and heath.

The flora of the wetland area includes marsh cinquefoil, marsh thistle, devil's bit scabious, greater bird's-foot trefoil and tufted vetch, but there is also an interesting mixture of rushes, sedges and grasses. Ferns such as hard fern, lemon-scented fern and common polypody grow on the hedge.

The drier eastern part of the reserve is open hay meadow, mown annually for the Trust by a local farmer. During high summer there's an attractive and colourful mix of flowers – yellow rattle, hardhead or knapweed, selfheal, meadow vetchling and lady's smock, to name but a few. Orchids are also frequent and common spotted and heath spotted have been identified to date.

To maintain the floral diversity of the hay meadow, the present annual mowing regime is essential. In the last few years numerous ditches and the main stream have been reinstated and are now maintained throughout the year. Attempts are being made to control the bracken.

The **Dalby Mountain Fields** upland reserve is 4.4 hectares (11 acres) and the mosaic of habitats supports a tremendous diversity of species. For example, in the fields over 100 plant species have been recorded, more than 96% of which are native to the Isle of Man. Notable species are common spotted, heath spotted and northern marsh orchids, crowberry, English stonecrop and round-leaved crowfoot (both of the latter having restricted distribution in the British Isles) and western gorse – a declining and globally-threatened species.

Species typical of marshland include sedges, bog asphodel, cotton-grass, devil's bit scabious, lousewort, marsh orchids, bog-bean (growing at its highest altitude on the island) and willows. Round-leaved crowfoot grows in puddles. The wet areas are excellent for invertebrates and a survey of these is being carried out. Common frog is also present. Bird species recorded on the reserve include skylark, curlew, swallow and meadow pipit.

The two fields of this reserve form part of a large grazing block, grazed by cattle for much of the year. The cattle make regular but not prolonged forays on to the reserve and this light grazing and trampling are ideal to maintain the site's great diversity of species.

Fell's Field (Lezayre) is 1.2 hectares (2.77 acres) in size, a pastureland habitat bound on three sides by Manx sod hedges which are topped by grey willow, blackthorn, elder and holly.

Prior to donation to Manx Wildlife Trust, the field was rented out for grazing but the Trust decided to embark on an ambitious project to create a wild flower meadow – achieved by cutting 4 of the meadows at Close Sartfield nature reserve to produce 47 large round bales and unrolling them at Fell's Field with the help of many volunteers. In line with the principles of haymaking, this hay was subsequently turned three times, ensuring that the wild flower

seeds fell on to the ground at Fell's Field rather than at Close Sartfield, thereby producing wild flowers for the following year.

Along the eastern edge of the field is a right of access. This has been fenced off and a hedge of native shrubs planted – hawthorn, hazel, blackthorn, elder, rose and rowan.

Ongoing management of the reserve initially saw the meadow cut for hay in late summer and, over winter months, grazed by sheep. But to combat an invasion of hogweed, which significantly reduces the field's diversity, this was revised so that (for as long as necessary) grazing takes place for most of the year and negates the need to cut the field.

At 16 hectares (42 acres), **Goshen** (Ballaugh) is one of the larger reserves, habitats comprising hay meadows, marshy grassland, curragh and developing woodland. Notable flora species are common and heath spotted orchid, northern marsh orchid, twayblade and yellow bartsia. Notable fauna species are hen harrier, curlew and corncrake, the latter observed on the reserve in 1999 and 2000. The reserve is on the western fringe of the Ballaugh Curragh and comprises twelve separate parcels of land – ten meadows and two areas of curragh (willow scrub) and developing woodland.

The flora is a diverse variety of meadow and wetland plants including yellow rattle, purple loosestrife, eyebright, yellow iris and knapweed. The fauna includes hare and the reserve is also notable as the haunt of the Manx robber-fly, the Latin name of which (*Epitriptus cowinii*) commemorates former Manx naturalist W.S. Cowin.

The reserve is effectively divided by a track, each of the two blocks fenced. Seven of the meadows are cut for hay in late summer, and sheep graze in winter. The two areas of curragh are left to develop naturally into woodland. Ditches are regularly cleared. Two meadows on the land purchased in

Marram grass at Jurby. This spot is close to Cooildarry Nature Reserve and its important woodland and river habitats described on page 82.

2008 are cut for hay but not grazed, and the remaining field is grazed by the local population of wallabies!

Lough Cranstal (Bride) is 2.27 hectares (5.6 acres), habitats comprising curragh (willow scrub), marshy grassland, and open water within an area of peat bog. Notable species are greater pond sedge, which is found nowhere else on the Isle of Man, and knotted pearlwort and water lily, both also rare and present at only a few other sites.

Lough Cranstal is a large wet area that was once a lake, thought to have formed about 8,000 years ago as a saltwater lagoon. As shingle ridges built up they cut it off from the sea. The salt water from the lagoon would have slowly drained away, but fresh water would have run into it from the Bride Hills to create a freshwater lake, as shown in a map dated 1860. A drain was cut some time after this and Lough Cranstal has been slowly drying out, leaving a boggy area, the drain emptying on to the Ayres near the Ayres Visitor Centre. In recent times it has not been used for farming and much of what was once grazing has reverted to impenetrable curragh.

The vegetation in the wet areas includes pondweeds, horsetail, white waterlily, knotted pearlwort and common sundew. In the marshy areas there are many types of sedge, including greater pond sedge and greater tussock sedge – the latter recorded on only a few sites outside the island's central valley curragh.

Attractive plants such as marsh marigold, lady's smock, ragged robin, meadowsweet and purple loosestrife are here, and on

Spectacular view of the the Chamas.

tussocks sticking out in the boggy areas are cotton-grass, heather and orchids. Five orchid species have been recorded: common twayblade, common spotted orchid, early marsh orchid, northern marsh orchid and heath spotted orchid. Three-spined sticklebacks have been seen in the peaty pools, and the rich invertebrate life and remoteness of the reserve attract many bird species. Currently, the site is unmanaged.

Miss Guyler's Meadow (Lezayre) is named after the donor and is a hay meadow habitat of 1.2 hectares (3 acres). Notable species are common spotted and heath spotted orchids. The meadow rises to a little eminence (or cronk) and is drier than many in the immediate vicinity. The high area of the meadow once formed part of a more elevated section of the Sulby Curragh, which was known as the Receiver's Island – an old name implying that in earlier times there was land here above flooded meadowland.

In late spring the field is coloured by bluebells and white flowering pignut, and in summer by blue harebells, and the trees and shrubs along the field margins are alive with the calls of many birds, notably the area's numerous curlews. The meadow is cut for hay in late summer and sheep graze it in winter.

Moaney & Crawyn's Meadows (Lezayre) is a reserve of 1 hectare (2.5 acres), leased since 1994 from Plantlife, the wild plant conservation charity, at a peppercorn rent. Habitats are traditional hay meadows, and notable species are pale sedge, greater butterfly orchid, royal fern and yellow bartsia.

Home to a variety of grassland and wetland species, these two fields are divided by a traditional Manx sod hedge which is lined with grey willow. Occurring along the hedge are fine clumps of royal fern, and pale sedge is notable as it is found in only a handful of sites in the island's north. Other plants present include common and heath spotted orchids, common knapweed, purple loosestrife, yellow rattle and meadow fescue. In the corner of one field is a patch of yellow flag.

The hay is cut in late summer and sheep graze the meadows in winter.

Wild in another sense – the sea pounding the spectacular scenery of the west coast.

To learn more about the Isle of Man visit:
www.lilypublications.co.uk